Dixie Witch

Dixie Witch

Dixie Witches: 9 True Southern Witch Trials

Text Copyright © 2017, by CL Gammon, All Rights Reserved

Dixie Witches: 9 True Southern Witch Trials

The cover illustration is a public domain image featured in *The History of Witches and Wizards* (1720).

Dixie Witches: 9 True Southern Witch Trials

For my sister, Wanda Clark

Acknowledgments

This book is the result a story my wife Kim showed me in the Macon County, Tennessee Historical Society Newsletter. It got me thinking about the topic of witch trials and one thing led to another. Of course, this is nothing new. Kim has always been there to aid me. I am eternally grateful to her.

Thanks to Shelta McCarter Shrum. Shelta ran down a newspaper report for me that I was having trouble finding. It would have been much more difficult to finish this book without her assistance.

Thanks to Sandra K. Gorin of the Barren County, Kentucky Historical Society for allowing me to reference an article that she wrote on a witch trial in Kentucky.

Acknowledgments notwithstanding, I, and I alone, am responsible for any errors that may be contained within the pages of this book.

Dixie Witches: 9 True Southern Witch Trials

Table of Contents

Introduction – Pages 1-4

1. America's First Witch Trial – Pages 5-8

2. Witchcraft and the Law – Pages 9-11

3. A Deathbed Accusation – Pages 12-15

4. Dunking a Witch – Pages 16-23

5. A Witch Trial in a Barn – Pages 24-30

6. A Bluegrass Witch Trial – Pages 31-38

7. Witches and the Bible – Pages 39-46

8. Were Witches Real? – Pages 47-52

9. A Preacher's Witch – Pages 53-57

10. An Alabama Witch Trial – Pages 58-61

11. A Tennessee Wizard – Pages 62-71

12. American Witch Doctors – Pages 72-73

13. Silver Bullets and Witches – Pages 74-75

14. The One-Eyed Witch – Pages 76-78

15. The "Old Hag Syndrome" – Pages 79-80

16. European Witch Trials – Pages 81-90

17. The Salem Myths – Pages 91-97

Conclusion – Pages 98-99

Sources Consulted – Pages 100-103

About the Author: Page 104

Other Books by CL Gammon: Pages 105-106

Dixie Witches: 9 True Southern Witch Trials

Introduction

"It were better that ten suspected witches should escape than that one innocent person should be condemned." – Increase Mather

Witchcraft is in vogue today. It is a subject of books, movies, and video games. For the most part, those producing today's fictional witchcraft lore have stripped it of any mention of Satan or evil. They present witchcraft as an expression of "white magic" which is used for good purposes. Today's witchcraft is vanilla, clean, and safe – suitable even for children.

Of course, most viewed witchcraft very differently in years past. Other generations saw witchcraft as an abomination; an expression of evil – something that society must protect against and stamp out.

When one considers witch trials, one will certainly conjure up thoughts of the events at Salem, Massachusetts in 1692 and 1693. However, here in the South there have been numerous trials of witches, wizards, and the like. In fact, southern witch trials predate those of New England.

This book is not about witch stories. It is a recounting of a few witch trials. Judges presided over some of these trials in courts of law; church officials conducted others. Some of those accused of witchery faced brutality and torture and some remained outcasts after their trials. On the other hand, many of the southern witches won their cases and some of them received damages from their abusers.

In those cases where the accused stood before church leaders and their respective congregations, the penalty for witchcraft was excommunication. One can argue that a church proceeding is not a trial, but most major sects (the Presbyterian for instance) refer to excommunication proceedings as trials. One must also remember that in centuries past, many considered separation from the church a very severe punishment indeed.

The author is not very interested in the specific activities of individuals accused of being witches. Of course, he had no choice but to relate the "evidence" witnesses gave against these men and women accused of bewitching their neighbors. This includes allegations of supernatural activities. However, if the reader expects fanciful stories of witches practicing their demented, demonic black arts, he will be disappointed.

The author *is* interested in the reactions of those who suspected witches in their midst. Thus, he looks closely at how persons behaved when confronted with the specter of witches in their communities. These reactions reveal a great deal about persons of that time – and of this time too.

The author had scores of cases from which to choose, but he made a point of concentrating on cases with which most readers are not well acquainted. Of course, in the communities in which these trials occurred, these cases are famous. There was no need to present many similar cases of witch trials. The nine cases related here are enough to give a good picture of witch trials in the American Southland.

Beyond the nine trials related here, the author has added several chapters amplifying upon the subject. These chapters will provide the reader with a feel for how our ancestors viewed witchery and how they attempted to combat it.

The author has placed these cases in chronological order. They span a period of more than two centuries. Where possible, the author depended upon official court and church documents in recounting these cases. He also relied upon letters, newspaper accounts and other materials produced at the time the cases took place. The author tried to remain detached, even-handed, and serious in the presentation of these cases. However, some of the witch trials contained humorous elements that he could not resist including.

Finally, the author reminds the reader that in the times these trials took place (between 1626 and 1859); a large number of people believed witchcraft was real and evil – the work of the Devil. To these people, a witch acting at the behest of the Devil was as real – and as dangerous – as any wild beast.

Sometimes the motivations of those accusing their neighbors of being witches had nothing to do witchcraft. Instead, many men and women faced accusations of witchcraft because someone wanted to do them harm and believed that a charge of witchery was the best means of achieving that purpose. One could debate whether fear and ignorance was more

Dixie Witches: 9 True Southern Witch Trials

justifiable than a mere attempt to gain revenge, but that is a discussion for another time.

1. America's First Witch Trial

The first witch trial considered here is older and better known than most of the other cases in this book. In fact, it was the first legally conducted witch trial in colonial America. It took place in Surry County, Virginia in the year 1626. This was sixty-six years before the Salem Witch Trials.

Joan Wright was a midwife (called a "goodwife" at the time). In addition to delivering babies, she aided her neighbors by curing their ills with folk remedies. She, her husband Robert, and their two children moved the forty miles or so from Kecoughtan to Surry County in 1625 or 1626. Evidently, the good folk of Kecoughtan had accused Joan Wright of witchery there before she and her husband moved to Surry County. It also appears that the accusations followed her to her new home.

On September 11, 1626, Lt. Giles Allington went before the Surry County Court and gave testimony accusing Joan Wright of witchcraft. The court took Allington seriously. He was a "substantial citizen of the colony" and he was a stockholder in the corporation that founded Virginia – the London Company.

Lt. Allington swore that he had spoken to goodwife Wright about being the midwife for his wife. However, his wife did not want Wright to be there. Joan Wright was left-handed and superstitious persons such as Mrs. Allington feared that left-handed persons were under the influence of the Devil.

Allington continued that he honored his wife's wishes and hired a Mrs. Gray to serve as midwife. He shared with the court that Joan Wright became "very much discontented" that he had chosen another midwife to help his wife deliver the baby.

Allington stated that after he refused to hire Wright, his household fell into misery. First, his wife breasts became "dangerously sore" and she did not recover for four or five weeks. Then, as soon as his wife recovered, he fell ill for three weeks. Then Allington made his most serious charge. He claimed that his baby became ill immediately after birth and the child continued to be sick for a month. The child experienced intense pain for another five weeks and then died.

The murder charge Allington leveled was not the only one made against Goodwife Wright. Rebecca Gray added to the charges. In fact, she implied that Wright had committed several other murders by witchcraft. Gray testified Wright told her she could cause the death of Mr. Gray by placing a token on his wife's forehead. In addition, Gray testified that (1) Wright had told a Mr. Felgate that his wife would die, and his wife did die. (2) Wright told Gray that Thomas Harris would soon "bury his wife" and his wife died a few days later. (3) Finally, Gray testified that Wright told her that a woman had said, "I have a cross man for a husband" and Wright responded, "Be content" because he would soon die, and it "came to pass."

Thomas Jones was the next to testify against Joan Wright. He said that a Sergeant Booth told him a story of Wright's witchery. It seems that Booth and Wright had an argument and afterwards he went hunting. Sergeant Booth related that although he saw "good game" at close range, "for a long time after he could never kill anything." Thus, he stated his opinion that Wright had bewitched his weapon.

Goodwife Wright had her defenders too. Her husband Robert testified that he and his wife had been married for sixteen years, but he knew nothing about "the crime she was accused of."

Isabella Perry followed Robert Wright to the witness stand. She testified that goodwife Wright had "railed against a girl of goodwife Yates for stealing . . . a log of light wood out of the fort." Upon this, goodwife Yates accused Joan Wright of being a witch and continued by accusing her of doing "many bad things" at Kecoughtan.

Perry said she asked Wright why she did not try "complain" and try to clear her name.

Wright made light of the encounter and responded simply, "God forgive them." However, goodwife Wright threatened the girl and told her that if she did not return the wood, she would cause her to dance naked. The next morning, the wood was back in its original place.

Alice Baylie testified next. She stated that she asked goodwife Wright if she would outlive Mr. Baylie. Wright responded that she knew the answer, but that she had been "exclaimed against for such things" and that she would never make such a prediction again.

The court considered the "evidence" against goodwife Wright – even though it was all either hearsay or supposition. After its deliberation, the court found Wright guilty. However, even though the charges against her included murder, the court handed down a very light punishment. It fined Joan Wright the sum of 100 pounds of tobacco.

After the trial, Joan Wright returned to her home and continued her life as if nothing had happened.

2. Witchcraft and Civil Law

As the events depicted above illustrate, Great Britain had strong laws against witchcraft in place. After England broke with the Roman Catholic Church, British monarchs and the Parliament continued to take witchcraft seriously. The English passed laws prohibiting witchcraft and punishing it with severe penalties, including death.

Blackstone, in his *Commentaries* under the heading, "Offenses Against God and Religion" wrote concerning these laws and other aspects of legal action against witches. Below are his remarks (the author has modernized Blackstone's spelling for the reader's convenience):

"A SIXTH species of offences against God and religion, of which our ancient books are full, is a crime of which one knows not well what account to give. I mean the offence of witchcraft, conjuration, enchantment, or sorcery. To deny the possibility, nay, actual existence, of witchcraft and sorcery, is at once flatly to contradict the revealed word of God, in various passages both of the old and new testament: and the thing itself is a truth to which every nation in the world hath in it's turn borne testimony, by either examples seemingly well attested, or prohibitory laws, which at least suppose the possibility of a commerce with evil spirits. The civil law punishes with death not only the sorcerers themselves, but also those who consult them; imitating in the former the express law of God, "thou shalt not suffer a witch to live." And our own laws, both before and since the conquest, have been equally penal; ranking this crime in the fame class with heresy, and condemning both to the flames. The president Montesquieu ranks them also both together, but with a very different view: laying it down as an important maxim, that we ought to be very circumspect in the prosecution of magic and heresy; because the most unexceptionable conduct, the purest morals and the constant practice of every duty in life, are not a sufficient security against the suspicion of crimes like these. And indeed the ridiculous stories that are generally told, and the many impostures and delusions that have been discovered in all ages, are enough to demolish all faith in such a dubious crime; if the contrary evidence were not also extremely strong. Wherefore it seems to be the most eligible way to conclude, with an ingenious writer of our own though one cannot give credit to any particular modern instance of it . . ."

". . . Our forefathers stronger believers, when they enacted by statute 33 Hen.VIII.c.8. all witchcraft and sorcery to be felony without benefit of clergy; and again by statute 1Jac.I.c.12. that all persons invoking any evil spirit, or consulting, covenanting with, entertaining, employing, feeding, or rewarding any evil spirit; or taking up dead bodies from their graves to be used in any witchcraft, sorcery, charm, or enchantment ; or killing or otherwise hurting any person by such infernal arts; should be guilty of felony without benefit of clergy, and suffer death. And, if any person should attempt by sorcery to discover hidden treasure, or to restore stolen goods, or to provoke unlawful love, or to hurt man or beast, though the fame were not effected, he or she should suffer imprisonment and pillory for the first offence, and death for the second. These acts continued in force till lately, to the terror of all ancient females in the kingdom: and many poor wretches were sacrificed thereby to the prejudice of their neighbors, and their own illusions; not a few having, by some means or other, confessed at the gallows. But all executions for this dubious crime are now at an end ; our legislature having at length followed the wife example of Louis XIV in France, who thought proper by an edict to restrain the tribunals of justice from receiving information of witchcraft. And accordingly it is with us enacted by statute 9 Geo.II. c.5. that no prosecution shall for the future be carried on against any person for conjuration, witchcraft, sorcery, or enchantment. But the misdemeanor of persons pretending to use witchcraft, tell fortunes, or discover stolen goods by skill in the occult sciences, is still deservedly punished with a year's imprisonment, and standing four times in the pillory."

First, the American colonies, and then the states of an independent America employed the British statutes on witchcraft against those they feared were sorcerers. In fact, American authorities continued to attempt to apply certain laws years after the British Parliament repealed them.

3. A Deathbed Accusation

The next case comes from Currituck, Albemarle County, North Carolina in 1703. It concerns the charges Deborah Bouthier made just before she died. Bourthier claimed that Susannah Evans had bewitched her and caused her agony. The case went before a Grand Jury.

The person who made a record of this case erroneously recorded it as taking place in 1697 under the reign of William III. However, from the indictment, one can tell that Queen Anne was on the throne when the Grand Jury considered the matter. The testimony puts the date the Grand Jury heard the case at 1703.

Below are the details of the case:

North Carolina's Royal Attorney General Richard Plater placed the indictment of Susannah Evans before the Grand Jury, under the witch law of James I.

The Grand Jury consisted of the following sixteen men: Cornelius Jones (foreman); Francis Beasley; William Erly; James Farlow; Cornelius Fitzpatrick; Zach Keeton; Robert Loury, William Luftman; Rich Madron; Hugh Pritchard; William Simson; Richard Stamp; Robert Wallis; James Ward; John Watkins; and John Worley.

The indictment read:

"The jurors for our Sovereign Lady, the Queen, present upon our oaths, that Susannah Evans of the precinct of Currituck, in the County of Albemarle, in the aforesaid Province, not having the fear of God before her eyes, but being led by the investigation of the Devil, did, on or about the twenty-fifth day of July last past, the body of Deborah Bouthier, being then in the peace of our sovereign lady, the Queen, and maliciously bewitch, and by assistance of the devil, afflict, with mortal pains, the body of the said Deborah Bouthier, whereby the said Deborah departed this life. And also did diabolically and maliciously bewitch several other of her Majesty's liege subjects, against the peace of our sovereign lady, the Queen, and against the form of the statute in that case made and provided."

Beyond the indictment, Thomas Bouthier gave a deposition and the Grand Jury reviewed it. In his deposition, Bouthier stated that on July 24, 1703 everyone in his household was in perfect health – except for one person. He continued that during that evening, he called for a servant named Thomas Walker, but Walker could not come. An affliction had struck Walker. The illness lingered with Walker for several months.

Bouthier swore that on the morning of July 25, Walker's wife returned from the home of John Evans to nurse her husband. That same morning, Bouthier's wife, Deborah, felt pain in her feet so extreme that she cried out in agony. After about 24 hours Deborah's foot pain receded, but she was "tormented in her bowels" for about a month. Deborah never recovered. She died in August of 1703.

According to Thomas Bouthier, while Deborah was suffering she accused the wife of

John Evans, Susannah, of witchcraft. Deborah Bouthier called Susannah Evans an "evil woman." Deborah claimed that Susannah caused all her suffering.

Some authors have speculated that Susannah Evans and Deborah Bouthier had "had words." However, there is no hard evidence that any argument between the women took place. Others have speculated that Bouthier had simply blurted out a name in her delirium. There is no definitive evidence of this either.

Regardless of her reasons, Thomas Bouthier stated that Deborah had asked him from her deathbed to have Susannah Evans "searched and examined" to prevent her from harming others. Generally, an "Able Jury of Women" from the community would search suspected witches for the mark of the Devil. There is no evidence that the court ordered a search of have Susannah Evans.

Thomas Bouthier completed his deposition by stating that before Deborah died, he had met with John and Susannah Evans in the presence of Thomas Vander Mullen and Richard Cominfort. (Bouthier said the Evans couple had compelled him to meet with them.) Bouthier continued that he told everyone present that he would honor the wishes of his ailing wife and then he repeated his charges that Susannah Evans was a witch. At that point, the enraged Evans couple "did abuse and threaten him"

The evidence of witchcraft presented by Attorney General Plater was too weak to earn an indictment. The Grand Jury reviewed the evidence and returned the following verdict:

"Wee of Ye Jury find no bill and ye person IGNORAMUS and it is Ordrd that the sd Sussnh Evens be acquitted pay the charges."

The Grand Jury did not employ the term "IGNORAMUS" in order to insult Thomas Bouthier. Ignoramus was a legal term (from the Latin for "we do not know"), which a grand jury could write on a bill when it considered the prosecution's evidence insufficient to bring an indictment.

Eventually, Susannah Evans received damages from Thomas Bouthier for besmirching her good name.

4. Dunking a Witch

The next southern witch trial explored is famous among those who follow witchery – not so for others. It was also one visited by more brutality than most witch trials in the Southland. The trial took place in Queen Anne County (currently Virginia Beach), Virginia in 1706.

Grace White Sherwood was middle aged and she had been married to a plantation owner named James Sherwood for more than two decades. Sherwood also sometimes acted as a midwife.

While she did not face charges until 1706, her neighbors had long suspected her of witchcraft. Sherwood may have found herself first accused as early as 1697, but the first recorded accusation occurred in 1698. In that year, John Gishburn accused her of bewitching his hogs and cotton. Sherwood and her husband sued Gishburn for slander, but did not prevail.

Later, Anthony Barnes accused Sherwood of riding his wife and then taking the form of a black cat and escaping through a keyhole. Sherwood sued Barnes as well, but again, the court refused to award her any damages.

Sherwood was a community nuisance and she had many ugly encounters with her neighbors. Sometimes the encounters became violent. In December 1705, Sherwood sued Luke Hill and his wife Elizabeth for assault and battery. This time she won her case in court.

However, she did not win very much. Grace Sherwood asked for 50 British Pounds, but received only 20 Shillings (1 Pound).

The Hills filed a lawsuit of their own on January 3, 1706. On that date, the Queen Anne County Court, presided over by a group of Justices of the Peace, heard the Hill couple charge Grace Sherwood with witchcraft. Some sources state that Elizabeth Hill charged Sherwood with causing her to miscarry, others state nothing more than that Hill accused Sherwood of bewitching her.

Although she knew Luke and Elizabeth Hill intended to charge her with witchcraft, Sherwood did not appear in court on that cold January morning. The justices ordered the Sheriff to compel Sherwood to appear at the next session of the County Court in February.

On February 6, 1706, Grace Sherwood was in court to answer the charges of witchcraft the Hills placed against her. The court took no action that day, but promised to take action the next morning.

On February 7, The County Court ordered that the Hills pay all fees associated with the trail. In addition, it ordered Sherwood to appear at the next session of the court and submit to a search by "An Able Jury of Women" to determine if Sherwood carried the "Mark of the Devil." After the search, the court would try Sherwood.

The County Court resumed on March 7. The Justices of the Peace of Queen Anne County listed as present on that date included: Edward

Moseley; Adam Thorrowgood; Henry Sprat; Horatio Woodhouse; John Cornick; Henry Chapman; William Smith; John Richardson; and George Hancock. However, the record does not list which of these nine men took part in the proceedings. Usually four of five justices made up a court.

The jury of twelve "ancient and knowing women" assigned to search Grace Sherwood were: Elizabeth Barnes (forewoman); Sarah Norris; Margaret Watkins; Hannah Dinnis; Sarah Goodarce; Mary Burgess; Sarah Sergeant; Winifred Davis; Ursula Henly; Ann Bridge; Ezable Waples; and Mary Cotle.

The women who searched Sherwood gave a report stating the suspected witch had on her body "Two things like titts" and several strange spots. While the search appeared to confirm that Sherwood carried the Mark of the Devil, which proved her a witch, the County Court declared there was nothing more it could do beyond initiating a petition to the Virginia General Court to take over the case.

The petition found its way to Virginia Attorney General Stevens Thomson on March 28, 1703. Thomson did not desire to pursue the matter. On April 16, Thomson informed the County Court that the petition was too general in nature and that it did not charge Sherwood with any specific act. The Attorney General opined that the county court should have incarcerated Sherwood and then the matter would have automatically come before the General Court.

Thomson suggested that the County Court reexamine the charges against Sherwood and if it found "cause to action" it should follow the law. Note: Double jeopardy was legal in Virginia at that time.

On May 2, the County Court took up the case against Grace Sherwood again. The court ordered the Sheriff to place Sherwood into custody until she could make bond. The court also ordered the Sheriff and a Constable to go to Sherwood's home and look for items that implicated her as a witch. The court tasked the Sheriff and Constable to look for clay or wax "images" of persons Sherwood might want to afflict.

It was a common belief that witches fashioned images out of clay or wax of those they wished to harm. Some even believed that witches presented the images to the Devil for disposition. Thus, finding wax or clay figures in a suspected witch's home was strong evidence indeed. Of course, the court would accept any evidence that made the case against Sherwood stronger. The Sheriff and Constable did not find anything proving that Sherwood was a witch.

The court also ordered the empanelling of another jury of women to examine Sherwood.

On June 6, the County Court tasked Maximillian Boush to act as the prosecutor in the case and ordered a regular trial.

On June 7, the court found it was having difficulty in finding a jury of women to examine Sherwood. The justices ordered the Sheriff to continue trying to find enough women to form a jury. In addition, the court ordered again that Sherwood remain in custody until she made bond.

On July 5, the County Court took up the matter once more. The Justices of the Peace trying the case were John Richardson, John Moseley, Henry Chapman, and William Smith. The justices still had not found a jury of women to examine Sherwood and they stated that it might no be possible to empanel a jury without compelling women to do it.

In order to settle the matter, the court asked Sherwood if she would agree to being "dunked" in a river to prove her either innocent or guilty. Sherwood consented allowing the authorities to dip her into a nearby river. However, the weather was rainy and unsettled. The justices feared that dunking her in the river at that time might endanger Sherwood's health. Instead, the court appointed a committee to go to the jail the next Wednesday at 10 a.m., take custody of Sherwood, and dunk her. This committee consisted of John Richardson and Henry Chapman.

On July 10, the court was finally ready to dunk the suspected witch. The authorities took Sherwood to the plantation belonging to John Harper and prepared her for dunking in the Lynnhaven River near what is today Virginia Beach, Virginia. The justices made a point of ordering the Sheriff to keep Sherwood from drowning.

Of course, a great crowd came out to attend the dunking of Sherwood. After all, how often does one have the opportunity to see a witch dunked in a cold, deep river on a warm summer's day?

The authorities, who had forced a group of women to agree to examine Sherwood, ordered her searched before she entered the water. This was to prevent her from doing anything to trick the judges. Then the Sheriff bound Sherwood to prevent her from wiggling out of her desperate situation.

Under the rules of dunking, if Sherwood sank, she was innocent. However, if she floated, she was a witch. Either her bindings slipped when they became wet, or she untied herself. Whatever happened, after being under the water for a few seconds, Sherwood's ropes came off, and she shot back to the surface of the water. This not only startled those looking on, it indicated to them that she was a witch.

After they brought Sherwood out of the water and returned her to shore, the justices took a short recess to consult with each other and to determine what the dunking proved. During the delay, the jury of women whom the court had forced to examine Sherwood preformed it mission. The court had ordered the women to "Search her Carefully For all teats spotts and about her body not usual on others . . ." The women were also tasked to search for any other evidence of the Mark of the Devil on Sherwood's body.

When the court reassembled, it concluded that there was a great deal of evidence against Sherwood and that "she could not make any excuse" for what everyone observed. While the dunking experience led the justices to believe that Sherwood was guilty, the report of the women who examined her clinched it. The old women swore that physically Grace Sherwood was not like them, or any other woman of which they had ever known. The women testified that Sherwood had "two things like titts on her private parts." The women continued that the things were black – blacker than the rest of her body.

Evidently, the women did not consider the fact that the drenched and shivering suspect was blue from her ordeal. They, nor the court, considered that her nipples would be darker than usual due to the cold water dunking.

Armed with all the evidence they needed, the justices found Sherwood guilty and ordered the Sheriff to place her in chains and hold her in jail until the General Court decided to try her. Evidently, General Court never put Grace Sherwood on trial.

Sherwood survived the ordeal. She was out of jail by sometime in 1708, or perhaps sooner. Some sources state inaccurately that she remained in prison until 1714. The proof that she was out of jail by 1708 is that she continued to be involved in lawsuits. In 1708, she lost a civil suit and the court ordered her to pay Christopher Cocke the sum of 600 pounds of tobacco.

Grace Sherwood lived among her accusers until her death in 1740. While she may not have been popular, she was no pauper either. The proof of this is the fact that when she died she left varying sums of money to her three sons, James, Richard, and John.

Note: The reason that persons in those days believed that a witch would not sink when dunked was simple. They believed that as a disciple of Satan, it was impossible to baptize a witch. Thus, the water would reject a witch and push it to the surface.

5. A Witch Trial in a Barn

One would think that by the end of the American Revolution our nation would have matured and evolved to the point that witch trials in the United States would have become a relic of the past. This is not the case. The "trial" related in this chapter took place in South Carolina in 1792 – the same year that George Washington won election to a second term as President of the United States.

The earliest known version of this trial comes from a manuscript written by an attorney named Philip Edward Pearson sometime before 1854. While second-handed, the manuscript and other documents give a fair account of what happened in this case.

In 1792, a plague descended upon South Carolina. Herds of cattle fell ill and died suddenly. In addition, yellow fever – which some people mistook for demonic possession – struck the population of the southern state hard and many persons died from it. What the good people of South Carolina did not know was that the epidemic they suffered was affecting most of the rest of the United States as well.

As the epidemic lingered and grew worse, the good people of Fairfield County, South Carolina believed that they had to solve their problem and end their misery. Some of them believed they had found the cause of their sorrows. There was a "strange" and "foreign" religious sect operating in the county called itself the Gifted Brethren. Those who did not understand the Gifted Brethren accused the sect of practicing hypnosis, of taking part in unorthodox customs, and of teaching a wrong interpretation of the Christian Trinity.

Some in South Carolina had suspected the Gifted Brethren for yeans. In 1761, Charles Woodmason, an Anglican minister in South Carolina, attacked several sects that had moved in from Pennsylvania. Woodmason called these sects "New Monsters." He wrote, "One of these Parties, known by the Title of New Lights or the Gifted Brethren (for they pretend to Inspiration) now infest the whole Back Country, and have even penetrated South Carolina." Woodmason did not like the idea of the Gifted Brethren "infesting" his state and he led unsuccessful efforts to eradicate them.

For years, rumors abounded that witches roamed throughout Fairfield County, but there was little or no action taken against the supposed practitioners of black magic. However, with the plague ravishing their community, some of the citizens of Fairfield County finally concluded they had to act. These citizens believed their agony was the result of witchcraft and that the Gifted Brethren were the witches causing the mischief. Several members of the sect found themselves accused of witchery. However, a German immigrant named Mary Ingleman drew most of the attention.

Mary Ingleman was a "neat, tidy and decent old lady. Her conversation was pleasant, entertaining, instructive; her manners mild, simple and agreeable." Apparently, Ingleman had knowledge of folk medicine. One person wrote, "Her application of simples in the cure of country complaints was the result of much observation and gratuitous practice . . ."

Mary's medical skills did not help her in this case. A vigilante group from Fairfield County "arrested" Mary, a man named Harding, his wife and an old woman named Sally Smith. This group of witch hunters placed the four on "trial." However, the trial was in no way legal.

The vigilante group simply rounded up the accused witches and housed them in a barn five miles south of Winnsboro, South Carolina (fifteen miles from Ingleman's home). The barn belonged to a local farmer named Thomas Hill. Hill served as the judge during the trial. The person Hill appointed "Sheriff" and "executioner" was a poor farmer named John Crossland. Hill evidently chose Crossland because the young man was strong and powerful. Thus, Crossland could handle the physical requirements of his position.

There were many willing to testify against the accused witches. Rosy Henley charged Mary Ingleman with putting a spell on her and her sister. The testimony revealed that Rosy, "Lying in her bed she could not be prevented by the utmost exertions of four strong men from rising up and clinging to the ceiling." The testimony continued that they "were both bitten on the neck and shoulders and stuck over with pins and splinters. Their case was dreadful . . ."

Mary Ingleman's son from a previous marriage, Adam Free, testified that his mother once asked him for one of his cows. He said that when he refused to give it to her, she became angry. He said Ingleman put a spell on the cow and caused it to rise into the air and then to fall back down to earth. The fall, according to him, broke the cow's neck.

Then Mary's grandson, Jacob Free, testified that Mary once transformed him into a horse and rode him the six miles to Pearson's apple orchard on Broad River. Jacob continued that while his grandmother filled her bag with apples, he decided to eat one as well. Jacob said that when Mary saw this, she struck him across the cheek. He said the blow made a long-lasting mark on his face.

Another witness against Ingleman was Martha Holley. Holley testified that Ingleman bewitched her and caused her to vomit up "balls of hair with pins sticking out, was all over the neck and shoulders stuck full of pins and splinters and deprived of all peace and comfort..."

However, Isaac Collins gave the most inflammatory testimony against Mary Ingleman. He charged her with consorting with Satan. Collins told the assemblage that once he was hunting deer in a field owned by a man named McTyre. Collins said he saw a deer and attempted to shoot it several times, but his rifle would not fire. Suspecting that a witch was preventing his cap and ball rifle from firing, he removed the lead ball, made a split in it, and inserted a sliver of silver into the split. He then testified that he fired his rifle again at the deer. The silver laden ball found its target, but instead of the deer falling, it transformed into a black cat. The cat, wounded in a front leg, limped away.

Next, Collins stated that a day or two later, he was plowing his field and he became thirsty and tired. He testified that he went to a spring near his field and after having a long drink of cold water, he sat beside the spring to rest. Collins continued that while he rested, Mary Ingleman walked up to him. She had an arm in a sling and she told him he was responsible for it. She also told him that she would not forget it.

Isaac Collins then testified that Ingleman transformed him in to a horse and rode him to a "Convention of Witches." Collins stated that he did not know the exact location of the convention, but that it was somewhere in North America.

Collins stated that during their ride to the convention, the Devil rode up beside her and said, "Mother Ingleman, you have a splendid horse."

"Ah," she responded, "This is that rascal Collins!"

Oddly, witnesses made charges against persons who avoided trial. One witness accused a man named Joe Fairs of causing Drury Walker's two children to float in the air. The story went that "It took four strong men to prevent her (the worse afflicted one) from rising out of her bed to the ceiling. Sometimes she would rise up the wall, slide across the ceiling and descend the opposite wall without injury . . ."

The accused witches offered no defense. Making a defense was pointless. The "jury" had determined the defendants were guilty before the trial began. Instead of pleading their cases, the defendants remained silent.

The jury voted the defendants guilty and then the punishment began. Crossland tied the victims to the barn's strong, wooden joists and flogged them mercilessly with his whip. Then he held the feet of the convicted witches "to a bark fire and confined [them] there until the soles popped off."

Finally, Crossland ended the torture and released the accused witches. Bloody from the beating, they limped toward their homes on their badly burned feet.

While the others made it back to their residences without incident, Sally Smith was not so lucky. A short distance from the Hill farm, a man came upon Sally, threw her down upon the ground, and placed a heavy pine log across her neck. Unable to free herself, Sally remained under the log all night long. Finally, sometime the next day a compassionate person found the old woman and removed the log.

After her ordeal, Mary Ingleman brought a civil suit against her persecutors. Reverend William Yongue, a Presbyterian minister, issued a warrant for John Crossland. A jury found Crossland guilty of assault and battery and fined him five pounds. However, Crossland never paid the fine. He left the county and went west to either Georgia or Alabama. None of the other persecutors faced any punishment.

The "justice" she received did not please Mary Ingleman. Although she remained in Fairfield County for the remainder of her life, she never forgave her antagonists.

6. A Bluegrass Witch Trial

As stated earlier, not all witch trials were civil or criminal in nature. Sometimes church congregations came together to make decisions about suspected witches. This case comes from Barren County, Kentucky. It began when a woman claimed that members of her church had falsely accused her of witchcraft.

On April 15, 1804, Mary Reynolds joined what is now the Green River Primitive Baptist Church at Amos Ferry (now Woodsonville) in Barren County, Kentucky. Mary was one of the earliest members of the church. The church had been in operation less than a year when Mary became a member.

After being a member of the church for almost a decade, in January 1813, at the monthly meeting of the church, a distraught Mary came forward and stated that three church members had accused her of practicing witchcraft. In those days, citizens took accusations of witchery seriously and a public accusation of witchcraft could damage a person's reputation permanently.

Being akin to Calvinists in faith, America's Primitive Baptist Churches are more closely related to the Puritan Church than they are to other fundamentalist churches doctrinally. An illustration of this similarity of beliefs is the doctrine of the "elect" held in common by both the Puritans and the Primitive Baptists.

However, to say that the Puritan doctrine had anything to do with the accusations against

Mary Reynolds would be incorrect. While John Calvin had supported the persecution of witches, that can also be said of almost every religious leader from the formation of the Roman Catholic Church, up until the late 19th century. In the early 19th century, most persons in the South – and the United States for that matter – believed in the demotic power of witches. To them witches were as real as any living being.

The charges of witchery were serious and church authorities could not ignore them. The leaders of the church called the accusers of Mary Reynolds before the congregation at the February 1813 meeting of the church. One of the accusers, a woman, made the charge before the church, but she refused give any reasons as to why she believed that Reynolds was a witch. However, she also refused to withdraw her charges. Finally, Mary's accuser asked to be "excluded" from the church and the church granted her wish.

Another accuser of Mary Reynolds was Thomas Logsdon. One person described Logsdon as a "man of moral courage and strong convictions . . ." Logsdon made his charges and maintained that everything he said was true.

Logsdon's remarks caused bedlam to break out in the church. Those supporting and opposing Reynolds shot accusations back and forth at each other, and the disturbance caused the church to conclude its services without reaching a decision.

At a later church meeting, Logsdon made more charges, but he could not support them with satisfactory facts and the church members voted to excommunicate him.

Reynolds faced charges before the church of "criminal and contradictory statements." However, at a later meeting, the church acquitted her of all charges.

Believing the church had exonerated her, and with her accusers no longer members of the church, Mary Reynolds thought her witch troubles had ended. However, she soon learned her troubles were far from finished.

There were members of the Green River church that were not satisfied with the outcome of the proceedings. Gossip and rumors filled the air. The story of this strange case spilled out into the community at large and soon people from miles around had heard the story of the suspected witch named Mary Reynolds.

The exaggerated story of the events inside the church caused Reynolds to become the villain in the court of public opinion and Thomas Logsdon to become the hero. The largely false story that developed was that Logsdon was a Godly and honest man, who a few corrupt "aristocrats" had ostracized, not because he lied about the witchery of Reynolds, but because he was a poor man.

Logsdon's supporters claimed that those supporting Reynolds had disrupted the church meeting preventing a true investigation of the witchcraft charge. They demanded the reinstatement of Logsdon. They also demanded that an honest investigation of Mary Reynolds and witchcraft take place.

The dispute continued throughout the summer and autumn of 1813 without abating. In fact, the argument grew more contentious by the day. Those opposing a witch trial claimed that witchcraft should not be a subject of investigation for persons of intelligence and learning. They thought it better to let the matter die. Leaders of other churches agreed that witch trials were a thing of an ignorant past, and that there was no place for it in an enlightened era. Those in the public who felt themselves enlightened also agreed that there was no need for a trial.

However, a majority of church members believed that witchcraft was real and that God had willed them to stamp it out, if possible. In addition, a large percentage of the population at large believed in witches and they wanted all witches identified and eliminated.

The opponents of a new trial claimed that the church's Articles of Faith did not include a provision for trying a witch. Church Pastor Jacob Locke, who also acted as the church Moderator, agreed that there was no such provision in the church's Articles of Faith. Those favoring a trial did not accept the verdict. They demanded an addition to the Articles of Faith that would allow them to hold a witch trial. They demanded that the congregation decide the issue by a majority vote at the next monthly meeting.

The congregation decided that the vote would be on the following question:

"Is it consistent with Divinity for the followers of Jesus Christ to believe there is such a thing as supernatural witchcraft, or to encourage the same belief?"

Pastor Locke had organized the Green River Primitive Baptist Church and he was the only pastor the church had ever had. However, he had never faced a situation like this before. He tried to be balanced and fair, but he clearly wished that the matter would end quickly. He also wished to avoid putting Mary Reynolds on trial. However, he could not simply deny the congregation its right to hold a trial.

Pastor Locke told the congregation that if the majority voted "yes" on the question, the church would try Mary Reynolds as a witch. If the majority voted "no" there would be no trial.

The congregation decided to hold the vote at the regular meeting of the church on Saturday December 25, 1813. The fact that the church scheduled the meeting on Christmas Day had no special significance. Christmas did not hold much import in those days. No state made Christmas a holiday until 1836, when Alabama passed such a law, and Christmas did not become a national holiday until 1870

The vote on the trial drew intense interest in both churches and among the public across the region. Everywhere one went in southern Kentucky and Northern Tennessee there was a buzz about the upcoming vote. Preachers delivered sermons about it, politicians gave speeches about it, and everyone from schoolchildren, to merchants, to farmers had strong opinions on the subject.

As stated earlier, Pastor Jacob Locke opposed the trial. He felt that the continuing debate was harming the church and was making the populace living along the Barren and Green Rivers a laughingstock. He attempted to keep the debate as civil and "Christian" as possible. In addition, for as long as he could, Locke refused to make any strong pronouncements on the subject. However, he realized that the vote would either settle the position of the church or break it in half. He prayed that his church would reject the idea of witchery and would hold together.

Although Locke tried to remain above the fray, those on both sides of the issue engaged in an ugly campaign to carry their view to victory. The pro-trial faction did not have any recognized leader, but those pushing for the trial believed they had a substantial majority of the congregation on their side.

Although they were very confident of victory, it is certain that the pro-trial forces were never as strong as they believed they were. There were several church members that agreed with the pro-trial position in public, but who opposed in private.

The leaders of the anti-trial forces were some of the same men their opponents had labeled as "aristocrats" earlier that year. These men included Richard J. Munford, Peter Rowlett, and Thomas Woodson. These men decided that their best chance to carry the day was to treat the affair as if it were a political election. They endeavored to identify every church member opposed to the trial and make sure they were present when the vote took place.

Pastor Locke remained low-key for as long as he could, but leaders lead and the preacher was a leader. He made it known to the congregation – and to the public – that on Friday, December 24, he would deliver a sermon at the church. He promised that during this sermon he would preach on the matter of a witch trial from a "Christian" point of view.

The announcement of Locke's decision to speak on the subject before the vote excited the entire area. A great many persons expressed interest in hearing the sermon, and those putting the event together expected a mammoth turnout. In fact, they did not expect the church building to be large enough to hold the entire crowd, so they made arrangements to seat persons outside, if necessary.

In the days leading up to his sermon, Pastor Locke visited with every member of the congregation at their homes, prayed with them, and insisted that they attend his sermon, regardless of how they felt about the witch trial. The Reverend encouraged every member of the congregation to listen to his sermon, pray about the issue, and then vote for or against the trial with a "good conscience."

Friday, December 24, 1813, was unseasonably warm – almost like an Indian Summer day. The wonderful weather boded well for the huge turnout for which Pastor Locke hoped. He was not disappointed. Persons – including a large number of Baptist, Methodist, and Presbyterian preachers – came from all around Kentucky and Tennessee to hear the sermon.

The crowd sat outside on wooden benches especially constructed for the occasion. Pastor Locke stood at the church's double doors and looked outward at the multitude of eager listeners. The preacher was still relatively young and his voice boomed throughout the river valley. He spoke for three hours and made every point biblically, historically, and logically against the belief in witchcraft.

Locke gave one of the best sermons anyone in the area had ever heard. When the preacher concluded his remarks, everyone listening understood that Mary Reynolds would never go to trial for being a witch.

The next day, the congregation made its choice as scheduled. There was little debate; there were no loud arguments; there was no disorder at all. Perhaps this was because that everyone understood that the fight was over. The vast majority of the congregation voted not to hold the witch trial and the matter died.

A few of the most pro-trial members did leave the church, but most remained and the other members treated them with respect and goodwill. There was never another call for a witch trial in the Green River Church, but a good number of members held to their views on witches and witchcraft for the remainder of their days.

7. Witches and the Bible

The Bible is the most important book in the Christian world. It refers to witchcraft, sorcerers, familiar spirits, and those under the spell of the devil in many verses. The Bible employs strong language against those individuals accused and it calls for strong punishment of suspected witches. The Bible even sanctions the death penalty for witches.

As they settled America, Englishmen brought the Bible with them. Many of these new Americans believed that this Bible was the literal word of God and that they had a duty to apply it literally. Thus, they believed that they should follow the biblical commandments concerning witchcraft with vigor.

Of course, this belief that it was a duty for Christians to punish witches extended to churches. Many, many churches took actions to punish members for practicing magic or other forms of witchcraft. However, often the results were similar to the case just related about Kentucky. It was more common for churches to acquit suspected witches than it was for churches to convict them.

Below are some of the better-known references to witches found in the Bible. All quotes are taken from the King James Version of the Bible.

2 Chronicles 33:6 – And he caused his children to pass through the fire in the valley of the son of Hinnom: also he observed times, and used enchantments, and used witchcraft, and dealt with a familiar spirit, and with wizards: he wrought much evil in the sight of the LORD, to provoke him to anger.

2 Kings 21:16 – And he made his son pass through the fire, and observed times, and used enchantments, and dealt with familiar spirits and wizards: he wrought much wickedness in the sight of the LORD, to provoke [him] to anger.

Acts 19:19 – Many of them also which used curious arts brought their books together, and burned them before all [men]: and they counted the price of them, and found [it] fifty thousand [pieces] of silver.

Deuteronomy 18:9-12 – When thou art come into the land which the LORD thy God giveth thee, thou shalt not learn to do after the abominations of those nations. There shall not be found among you *any one* that maketh his son or his daughter to pass through the fire, *or* that useth divination, *or* an observer of times, or an enchanter, or a witch, Or a charmer, or a consulter with familiar spirits, or a wizard, or a necromancer. For all that do these things *are* an abomination unto the LORD: and because of these abominations the LORD thy God doth drive them out from before thee.

Galatians 5:19-21 – Now the works of the flesh are manifest, which are *these*; Adultery, fornication, uncleanness, lasciviousness, Idolatry, witchcraft, hatred, variance, emulations, wrath, strife, seditions, heresies, Envyings, murders, drunkenness, revellings, and such like: of the which I tell you before, as I have also told *you* in time past, that they which do such things shall not inherit the kingdom of God.

Isaiah 47:8-14 – Therefore hear now this, thou that art given to pleasures, that dwellest carelessly, that sayest in thine heart, I am, and none else beside me; I shall not sit as a widow, neither shall I know the loss of children: But these two things shall come to thee in a moment in one day, the loss of children, and widowhood: they shall come upon thee in their perfection for the multitude of thy sorceries, and for the great abundance of thine enchantments. For thou hast trusted in thy wickedness: thou hast said, None seeth me. Thy wisdom and thy knowledge, it hath perverted thee; and thou hast said in thine heart, I am, and none else beside me. Therefore shall evil come upon thee; thou shalt not know from whence it riseth: and mischief shall fall upon thee; thou shalt not be able to put it off: and desolation shall come upon thee suddenly, which thou shalt not know. Stand now with thine enchantments, and with the multitude of thy sorceries, wherein thou hast laboured from thy youth; if so be thou shalt be able to profit, if so be thou mayest prevail. Thou art wearied in the multitude of thy counsels. Let now the astrologers, the stargazers, the monthly prognosticators, stand up, and save thee from these things that shall come upon thee. Behold, they shall be as stubble; the fire shall burn them; they shall not deliver themselves from the power of the flame: there shall not be a coal to warm at, nor fire to sit before it.

Isaiah 8: 19 –And when they shall say unto you, Seek unto them that have familiar spirits, and unto wizards that peep, and that mutter: should not a people seek unto their God? for the living to the dead?

Leviticus 19:31 – Regard not them that have familiar spirits, neither seek after wizards, to be defiled by them: I am the LORD your God.

Leviticus 20:27 – A man also or woman that hath a familiar spirit, or that is a wizard, shall surely be put to death: they shall stone them with stones: their blood [shall be] upon them.

Leviticus 20:6 – And the soul that turneth after such as have familiar spirits, and after wizards, to go a whoring after them, I will even set my face against that soul, and will cut him off from among his people.

Revelation 21:8 – But the fearful, and unbelieving, and the abominable, and murderers, and whoremongers, and sorcerers, and idolaters, and all liars, shall have their part in the lake which burneth with fire and brimstone: which is the second death.

Revelation 22:15 – For without [are] dogs, and sorcerers, and whoremongers, and murderers, and idolaters, and whosoever loveth and maketh a lie.

Saul and the Witch

The most complete story of a major biblical figure meeting with a witch is found in book of 1 Samuel. Early English settlers in America took this story as a cautionary tale.

We pick up the story in 1 Samuel, Chapter 28, verse 3 and quote through verse 19:

3: Now Samuel was dead, and all Israel had lamented him, and buried him in Ramah, even in his own city. And Saul had put away those that had familiar spirits, and the wizards, out of the land.

4: And the Philistines gathered themselves together, and came and pitched in Shunem: and Saul gathered all Israel together, and they pitched in Gilboa.

5: And when Saul saw the host of the Philistines, he was afraid, and his heart greatly trembled.

6: And when Saul enquired of the Lord, the Lord answered him not, neither by dreams, nor by Urim, nor by prophets.

7: Then said Saul unto his servants, Seek me a woman that hath a familiar spirit, that I may go to her, and enquire of her. And his servants said to him, Behold, there is a woman that hath a familiar spirit at Endor.

8: And Saul disguised himself, and put on other raiment, and he went, and two men with him, and they came to the woman by night: and he said, I pray thee, divine unto me by the familiar spirit, and bring me him up, whom I shall name unto thee.

9: And the woman said unto him, Behold, thou knowest what Saul hath done, how he hath cut off those that have familiar spirits, and the wizards, out of the land: wherefore then layest thou a snare for my life, to cause me to die?

10: And Saul sware to her by the Lord, saying, As the Lord liveth, there shall no punishment happen to thee for this thing.

11: Then said the woman, Whom shall I bring up unto thee? And he said, Bring me up Samuel.

12: And when the woman saw Samuel, she cried with a loud voice: and the woman spake to Saul, saying, Why hast thou deceived me? for thou art Saul.

13: And the king said unto her, Be not afraid: for what sawest thou? And the woman said unto Saul, I saw gods ascending out of the earth.

14: And he said unto her, What form is he of? And she said, An old man cometh up; and he is covered with a mantle. And Saul perceived that it was Samuel, and he stooped with his face to the ground, and bowed himself.

15: And Samuel said to Saul, Why hast thou disquieted me, to bring me up? And Saul answered, I am sore distressed; for the Philistines make war against me, and God is departed from me, and answereth me no more, neither by prophets, nor by dreams: therefore I have called thee, that thou mayest make known unto me what I shall do.

16: Then said Samuel, Wherefore then dost thou ask of me, seeing the Lord is departed from thee, and is become thine enemy?

17: And the Lord hath done to him, as he spake by me: for the Lord hath rent the kingdom out of thine hand, and given it to thy neighbour, even to David:

18: Because thou obeyedst not the voice of the Lord, nor executedst his fierce wrath upon Amalek, therefore hath the Lord done this thing unto thee this day.

19: Moreover the Lord will also deliver Israel with thee into the hand of the Philistines: and to morrow shalt thou and thy sons be with me: the Lord also shall deliver the host of Israel into the hand of the Philistines.

The Bible continues that Saul paid a high price for consorting with the witch.

1 Chronicles 10:13-14 – So Saul died for his transgression which he committed against the LORD, [even] against the word of the LORD, which he kept not, and also for asking [counsel] of [one that had] a familiar spirit, to enquire [of it]; And enquired not of the LORD: therefore he slew him, and turned the kingdom unto David the son of Jesse.

1 Samuel 25:23 – For rebellion [is as] the sin of witchcraft, and stubbornness [is as] iniquity and idolatry. Because thou hast rejected the word of the LORD, he hath also rejected thee from [being] king.

Armed with the biblical prohibitions of witchcraft, and the story of Saul, Englishmen in the New World were certain that they should have no contact with witches – beyond punishing them. In addition, they believed that when they did locate witches among them, the punishment they imposed should be rough.

8. Were Witches Real?

For centuries, a debate has raged as to whether or not biblical authors believed that witches actually possessed magical powers. There have always been those who claimed that the Bible condemned witchery because those practicing it were mere charlatans and swindlers. According to these scholars, the Bible was not interested in battling against true sorcery, because there was no such thing. These scholars contend that biblical authors understood that those faking magical power could deceive and delude others and lead them to Satan and into sin.

Others claim that the Bible was clear that the Devil would empower witches to perform all sorts of magic in exchange for their doing his bidding. These commentators contend that the persecution of suspected witches came from a literal interpretation of the Bible.

Regardless of one's opinion on the matter, the leaders of the early Roman Catholic Church believed that the Bible told them that witches were real and dangerous. In addition, early Church leaders believed that witchcraft tainted those Christians (heretics) who stood in opposition to the Catholic faith. This made sense to the Catholics. They believed that both witches and heretics had contracted with the Devil to aid him in his diabolical interference in human affairs.

The joint desire to drive out witches and defeat heretics led to some of the most horrible events associated the Inquisition. Then, when the Protestants came to fore, they continued to believe that witches were real and that witches could – with the aid of Satan – do all kinds of impossible things.

Catholics and Protestants alike pointed to one indisputable fact as proof that witches were real – the confessions of suspected witches themselves. Of course, authorities extracted many confessions by the use of torture. However, many other times, persons under no suspicion came to authorities and confessed to being witches. These self-professed witches offered spontaneous confessions to all kinds of horrible acts.

One interesting case of a voluntary confession took place in the ninth century. In the Italian town known today as Benevento, a plague was destroying all the livestock. Unable to find a natural cause for the plague, the townspeople came to suspect witchcraft. Eventually, the citizens of the town accused a nobleman of paying men to spread some strange poison dust among the flocks and herds in order to infect the livestock.

When authorities took the men suspected of doing the bidding of the nobleman's into custody, they confessed immediately. Even though authorities may have spared them if they recanted, the men continued to declare they were guilty even as the executioner put them to death.

Cases of innocent persons confessing to crimes are common. Psychologists think that those most likely to confess to crimes they did not commit are persons suffering from mental illness or intellectual disability. Of course, in past ages authorities viewed the manifestations of mental illness as just another symptom of demonic possession. Thus, anyone displaying signs of mental illness stood a good chance of suffering conviction for witchcraft.

The Witchcraft Act of 1735

As time passed, more and more persons concluded that those claiming to possess magical powers were simply deceiving others. This being the case, the English passed a law in 1735 that reversed the legal view of witchcraft in Great Britain. First, the law repealed the act of King James against conjuring, enchanting, and practicing witchcraft and sorcery. The statute also prevented anyone from initiating a lawsuit against a suspected witch.

The British Parliament also recognized that some would continue to pretend to be witches and it intended to employ the Witchcraft Act of 1735 to stop the pretenders. The Parliament understood that pretended witches had the ability to delude and defraud "ignorant" persons. Thus, it made it a crime for anyone to pretend to exercise any "occult or crafty Science" to enchant, to conjure, to tell fortunes or to find treasures.

A person convicted of pretending to be a witch was subject to a year in jail. Despite the fact that the British repealed the witchcraft laws in 1735, some Americans (as we shall see) attempted to apply those laws for more than a century after the English expunged them.

The text of the Witchcraft Act of 1735 follows below:

"An Act to repeal the statute made in the first year of the reign of King James the First, intitutled, An Act against conjuration, witchcraft, and dealing with evil and wicked spirits, except so much thereof as repeals an Act of the fifth year of the reign of Queen Elizabeth, Against conjurations, inchantments and witchcrafts, and to repeal, an Act passed in the parliament of Scotland in the ninth parliament of Queen Mary, intituled, Anentis witchcrafts, and for punishing such persons as pretend to exercise or use any kind of witchcraft, sorcery, inchantment, or conjuration.

"Be it enacted by the King's most Excellent Majesty, by and with the Advice and Consent of the Lords Spiritual and Temporal, and Commons, in this present Parliament assembled, and by the Authority of the same, That the Statute made in the First Year of the Reign of King James the First, intituled, An Act against Conjuration, Witchcraft, and dealing with evil and wicked Spirits, shall, from the Twenty-fourth Day of June next, be repealed and utterly void, and of none effect (except so much thereof as repeals the Statute made in the Fifth Year of the Reign of Queen Elizabeth intituled, An Act against Conjurations, Inchantments, and Witchcrafts).

"II. And be it further enacted by the Authority aforesaid, That from and after the said Twenty-fourth Day of June, the Act passed in the Parliament of Scotland, in the Ninth Parliament of Queen Mary, intituled, Anentis Witchcrafts, shall be, and is hereby repealed.

"III. And be it further enacted, That from and after the said Twenty-fourth Day of June, no Prosecution, Suit, or Proceeding, shall be commenced or carried on against any Person or Persons for Witchcraft, Sorcery, Inchantment, or Conjuration, or for charging another with any such Offence, in any Court whatsoever in Great Britain.

"IV. And for the more effectual preventing and punishing of any Pretences to such Arts or Powers as are before mentioned, whereby ignorant Persons are frequently deluded and defrauded; be it further enacted by the Authority aforesaid, That if any Person shall, from and after the said Twenty-fourth Day of June, pretend to exercise or use any kind of Witchcraft, Sorcery, Inchantment, or Conjuration, or undertake to tell Fortunes, or pretend, from his or her Skill or Knowledge in any occult or crafty Science, to discover where or in what manner any Goods or Chattels, supposed to have been stolen or lost, may be found, every Person, so offending, being thereof lawfully convicted on Indictment or Information in that part of Great Britain called England, or on Indictment or Libel in that part of Great Britain called Scotland, shall, for every such Offence, suffer Imprisonment by the Space of one whole Year without Bail or Mainprize, and once in every Quarter of the said Year, in some Market Town of the proper County, upon the Market Day, there stand openly on the Pillory by the Space of One Hour, and also shall (if the Court by which such Judgement shall be given shall think fit) be obliged to give Sureties for his or her good Behaviour, in such Sum, and for such Time, as the said Court shall judge proper according to the Circumstances of the Offence, and in such case shall be further imprisoned until such Sureties be given."

9. A Preacher's Witch

To a large degree, the best history of rural Tennessee exists in local church records. The next trial in this collection comes from what is now Macon County, Tennessee. According to church records, the trial took place in the autumn of 1817. It began when Mary "Polly" Louise Gilliam Webb came under accusations of witchcraft.

Polly Webb belonged to the Testament Primitive Baptist Church. This church was of the same sect as the Green River Church of Kentucky considered in Chapter 6. Again, there is no evidence that the fact that the Testament Church shared some similarities to the Puritan church of the 17th century had anything to do with this church trial. However, it is interesting that several Primitive Baptist churches conducted witch trials in the 19th century.

It is unknown if anyone from the Testament Church listened to the sermon Reverend Locke gave in Kentucky in 1813. If so, it does not appear that the sermon had any influence on the congregation of the Tennessee church.

Polly Webb was 35 when on Saturday, October 11, 1817, several members of the Testament Primitive Baptist Church brought charges of witchcraft against her. The fact that Polly's husband was a man of the cloth only compounded the problem.

Testament Primitive Baptist Church is the oldest continuously active church in Macon County, Tennessee. Its founders organized it on

Saturday, February 8, 1812 – three decades before the founding of Macon County. Ironically, there is a strong possibility that its mother church was the "Salem Church" of Sumner County, Tennessee.

Her accusers made six charges against Polly Webb (and a single charge against her husband Daniel). One could interpret the meaning of the charges listed in the church record in several ways. Instead of offering an interpretation as to what the charges mean, the author lists them below verbatim so the reader may draw his own conclusions:

"No. 1 charge that Polly Webb, wife of Daniel Webb, member of the Baptist Church did say that she did take of witchcraft.

"No. 2 - That said Polly Webb was going from Isaac Dillons on a certain day - that she was so confused that she crossed the road six times without seeing it. Terry said, "How could she know that she crossed the road six times when she did not see it."

"No. 3 - Charge that on the same day while on her way home, her creature saw something and that said Polly wished she could see what the creature saw, and there appeared two little black things on each side of the path to whom she spake as follows: 'You think to scare me but you cannot - I know who you are and if you don't give me the way I'll turn you into your right shapes and show who you are' and when asked by a certain person if she could turn them into their right shapes, Polly replied, 'Yes I can and will if they don't let me alone.'

"No. 4 - Charge that Polly stated that a witch could not look her in the face and then denied it.

"No. 5 - Charge that Polly stated that she took witchcraft off of a horse.

"No. 6 - Charge that Polly stated that she made a woman sit still for 2 hours to punish her and then speaking low to said witch commanded her to go to the table and take up the candle who obeyed and gave the candle a whirl and went out of doors and returned no more.

"Charges were also made against Brother Webb for defending his wife."

Notes:

(1) The Isaac Dillon mentioned in charge #1 was from North Carolina originally. He was a Quaker by birth. Dillon owned a 150-acre farm in the Long Creek community of what was then Sumner County, Tennessee, but later became a part of Macon County.

(2) The "Terry" mentioned in charge #1 could have been one of the following: George Terry, Hannah Terry, or Mary Ann Terry. The three persons mentioned above were charter members of the Testament Church and attended its organization on February 8, 1812.

The Testament Primitive Baptist Church took a calm and prudent approach to the charges against Polly Webb. On Saturday, December 13, 1817, the congregation heard the witchcraft charges against her. The records of the church indicate that "After a patient and deliberate investigation of the subject, the church with the help of the aforesaid, are of the opinion that she be returned to her seat in Church."

From the above we can gather that Polly Webb acknowledged some wrongdoing and had asked for, and received, forgiveness from the other members of the church. However, the evidence does not indicate that Polly actually admitted to being a witch.

The problems Daniel and Polly Webb faced did not subside. Church records indicate that on Saturday, May 9, 1818, Daniel Webb "gave up care of the Church." The church dismissed him by a letter dated June 12, 1819.

On February 7, 1819, the church excluded Polly Webb from the congregation "for unchristian like spirit after being dealt with by several of the members trying to persuade her to make acknowledgements as she was first in the transgression. She decided not to forgive them nor have fellowship with them . . ."

Daniel and Polly Webb soon departed the area, moved to Henderson County, Tennessee and settled near the town of Lexington. The direct reasons for their departure are open to conjecture, but their bitter experiences with the Testament Primitive Baptist Church may have played a role.

The citizens of their new home did not hold the charges of witchery against Polly Webb. Daniel Webb served as the "principle preacher" at the Hepzibah Baptist Church in Henderson

County for many years. Polly Webb was a faithful churchgoer for the balance of her life.

Daniel Webb died on March 22, 1855 at the advanced age of 75. Polly Webb died on October 8, 1858. She was also 75. This author has found no evidence that anyone ever brought an accusation of witchcraft against Polly Webb again.

10. An Alabama Witch Trial

This case comes from 1821. It happened in the north Alabama town of Moulton. The famous woman journalist Anne Royall was a witness to the trial and she mentioned it a book she wrote. James Edmonds Saunders mentioned in a book he authored as well.

The story is sketchy, but there are several facts upon which all the sources agree. There was a young woman who took ill from a strange and unknown illness. This woman threw up everything she attempted to eat – and more. She threw up "knots of pins" and "hair." She felt excruciating pain and could not rest day or night.

The woman claimed that a neighbor woman had bewitched her. After weeks of continued sickness and more and more claims, the sick woman had convinced most of the local women that a witch was at work. Even the medical doctors became involved. These men of medicine conceded that the young woman was suffering from some supernatural ailment that no earthly medicine could cure.

The accused woman lived on the Flint River. She was poor and friendless. At first, the locals spoke of her witchery in whispers, but after the sick woman bombarded them for days with her witch story, the accusations grew louder.

Finally, a magistrate named David Knott, who lived near Oakdale, Alabama, issued a warrant for the accused supposed witch's arrest. The next day when the Sheriff presented the accused witch to the magistrate Knot a crowd of hundreds of townspeople where on hand to see the spectacle. Beyond that, several other local women came forth and said they were willing to testify that they too were bewitched.

Knot believed in witchcraft, but there was nothing presented to the court that moved him until the sick woman, who was very pale and thin, testified. The woman appeared very weak as she staggered to the witness stand, but she made it, finally. She gathered herself and testified that she was doing her laundry in the creek one day when she became very tired. Unable to continue with her washing, she sat on a beech tree root to rest.

Then the witness told an astonished court that the accused woman came down from the beech tree in the form of a squirrel with its tail curled over its back. The witness continued that the witch-squirrel barked a spell upon her and that she had been sick since. Just to clinch her testimony, the sick woman gave a vivid account of vomiting up hairballs and other things.

The appearance of the sick woman and her testimony moved the judge. He stated that he now had proof positive of the witchery and that he would order the prisoner confined in jail.

Most of the more sensible members of the audience sat in "dumb amazement" at the idea of a woman being incarcerated based on such farcical testimony.

Before the magistrate could complete his order, the County Clerk, a man named John Gallagher, rose and asked to address the court. Gallagher was a "young Irishman" who spoke perfect English in a flawless American accent. He was small; he had dark, fine hair; and his eyes were dark blue. Despite his stature, Gallagher had a commanding way about him.

Knot told Gallagher that he could say anything he wanted, and the young Irishman responded, "Then sir, allow me to remind you that it would be useless to send the woman to jail. For, if she is really a witch, she can escape through a keyhole; and if she should be innocent, it would be a great pity for her to be sent to prison."

The befuddled magistrate agreed that there was no way to hold a witch in a jail cell if she did not wish it, but he was at a loss as to what to do. Knot replied, "That's so! That's so!" "But what shall we do with her?"

Gallagher suggested that the magistrate release the suspected witch until the next convening of the Grand Jury, then the matter would fall to it. The judge liked the idea of allowing some other body to deal with the Moulton Witch. He adopted Gallagher's suggestion, released the suspected witch, and adjourned his court in short order.

The poor, sick woman grew worse and throughout the countryside men and women lamented the fact that the authorities were allowing the witch to continue to torment her. Some of the local men began planning to mount a raid upon the accused woman's house and to extract vigilante justice.

Before a mob descended upon the accused witch, someone discovered the true cause of the bewitching. It seems that the sick woman's husband had purchased a large barrel of brandy just before she became ill. The woman had a taste for brandy and drank as much of it as she could each day. Her constant intoxication caused her illness. The townsfolk were now angry with those who had misled them. They demanded that the man get rid of the brandy and he did. The wife, now sober, recovered from her illness.

A judge found the woman who cried "Witch" guilty of slander and levied a settlement against her. Finding themselves ostracized by the community, the woman and her husband left the area and never returned. No one bothered the so-called Moulton Witch again.

11. A Tennessee Wizard

This incident took place in Jamestown, Fentress County, Tennessee around 1830. This may the only time in Tennessee history that authorities took legal action against a suspected witch in a court of law. While the majority of American witch trials took place against females – legal actions taken against men accused of witchery were more common than some imagine.

Residents of the small town of Jamestown in East Tennessee grew suspicious of a little, "misshapen" old man named Obed (sometimes referred to as "Joe") Stout. Stout was a recluse, he did not attend church, and he sat up late at night and read "strange books." Of course, the above attributes were enough to convince many that Stout was partaking in Black Arts.

The citizens of Jamestown had been leery of Stout for some time and their suspicions of him grew stronger in the autumn of 1830. At that time, several girls and women in Fentress County suffered from a strange, unknown affliction. The symptoms of this illness included jerks, trembling, and "other ills that flesh is heir to . . ." The aliment stumped local doctors and although they endeavored diligently, they could do little to aid their patients. This led some of the locals to conclude that the sickness was the result of something supernatural – perhaps even witchcraft.

After suffering for several months, all the sick recovered, except for Rebecca French. French was older than most of those who suffered from the unknown illness. She was about forty and she had never been married. Since she did not improve her father, J. French, called in the best "witch doctors" from the surrounding area and they visited with Rebecca several times, but could not heal her.

Two of the witch doctors the French family called in to aid Rebecca where rather famous men – Isaac Taylor and his son Pleasant Taylor. The two had gained renown for driving out witches and for curing those under the "malign influence" of witchcraft. In this case, however, they had no more success in finding a cure for Rebecca than any of the other medical men or witch doctors.

Then, in January 1831, the French household received a visitor, Obed Stout. When Stout, who was the leading suspect in the bewitching of Rebecca, appeared at French home, Rebecca's father was surprised, but he allowed the little man to enter. Stout carried a rope he had fashioned from split buckeyes. When Stout came near Rebecca, her condition grew worse immediately and she jerked and trembled very violently.

Rebecca believed that the buckeye rope possessed the key to her cure and she asked Stout to give it to her. Stout declined at first, but when the men folk present threatened violence upon him if he did not give it to her, he relented. When she placed the rope around her waist, Rebecca was relieved of her symptoms immediately.

Those present believed they had proof positive that the little wizard was bewitching poor Rebecca. However, they determined that the buckeye belt was not a permanent cure. Only Stout could cure Rebecca completely. Rebecca's friends and family moved off to a corner of the room and discussed the matter. They decided that if Stout took Rebecca's hand, and spoke certain mysterious words, her affliction would disappear, and she would be immune to witchery for ninety-nine years!

However, before Rebecca's guardians decided upon a course of action, Stout slipped away from the French house and returned home. In order to force Stout to cure Rebecca, a man named Charles Staunton filed an "account" before a magistrate named French (almost certainly, this magistrate was Rebecca's father). Magistrate French issued a bail warrant and a constable deputized five others to act as a posse. The six men, armed with weapons possibly loaded with silver bullets, set out to arrest Stout. The posse located Stout, took him into custody roughly, and hauled him before French for trial.

The house where the "trial" took place was packed with friends, neighbors, and interested onlookers. After all, how many times does one get the opportunity to see a real-life wizard?

When they brought Stout before Rebecca, her symptoms grew even worse than before. In order to relieve her pain, each person in the house (except for Stout) took a turn in taking Rebecca by the hand and saying, "May the Great God in Heaven, in the name of the Father, Son and Holy Ghost, bless you."

However, this did not improve Rebecca's condition.

Stout was standing near the door in the back of the room. He was more interested in his own fate than in what was happening to Rebecca. Finally, a desperate Rebecca called to him, "Oh, Mr. Stout, bless me, I know you can relieve me." However, Stout made no move toward her. Rebecca's father also pleaded with Stout, but he still refused to help.

Finally, one of the members of the posse knocked the old man down with a chair and others threatened to shoot Stout if he did not give aid the ill woman. Faced with the prospect of death, the little wizard relented. He went up to Rebecca, took her by the hand, and spoke a few "mystic words." With that, Rebecca "was herself again, to the astonishment of all present . . ." If they were not convinced before, those witnessing the scene were now certain that "Stout had dealings with the 'evil one.'"

The case of the misshapen wizard led to several lawsuits. A few days after her recovery, Rebecca French took out a warrant against Stout charging him with witchcraft. For his part, Stout took out a warrant against Isaac Taylor, Pleasant Taylor, Charles Staunton, and others charging them with assault.

The weather was cold and fearful in Fentress County that winter. However, all the parties involved in the lawsuits trudged about twenty-five miles through high snowdrifts to a magistrate's home so that he could adjudicate the various claims. The magistrate determined that Stout was indeed a wizard and that he was in no danger from human hands. The magistrate then placed Stout under a $2,000 bond in the matter of bewitching Rebecca and ordered him to appear before at the next session of the Fentress County Court.

Stout was enthusiastic to prove his innocence. In February 1831, he appeared before the County Court and declared that he was ready for trial. However, Rebecca French did not appear in court to testify against him and the judge found Stout "not guilty." The judge also ordered Rebecca to pay court costs.

In May 1831, Isaac Taylor stood trial for his assault upon Stout. Taylor entered a plea of "not guilty." After the court empanelled a jury, the trial began.

Stout testified for the prosecution and he related his version of the events from the previous fall and winter. Stout described the abuse he suffered at the hands of Taylor and the other witch hunters.

Rebecca French's father testified for Taylor. J. French admitted that someone attempted to knock Stout down with a chair while the accused wizard was in the French home. However, French testified that no one took any other physical action against Stout.

French continued that he had never believed in witchcraft before Rebecca came down with her illness. French then acknowledged that he no longer doubted the existence of witchcraft. At that point, French shook his fist at Stout, called him a "very old sinner," and accused him of being a witch.

Pleasant Taylor testified on behalf of his father. The younger Taylor stated his firm belief in witchcraft. He testified he came to believe in witchcraft while hunting. Taylor said he "shot a deer with its right side towards him; that if fell at the crack of the gun, and when he examined the carcass, he found that the ball had entered on the left side, and lodged against the skin of the right side." This set of circumstances led Taylor to recognize the influence of some evil spirit.

After hearing the case, the enlightened jury found Taylor guilty and ordered him to pay damages.

Another Version of the Story

While there is documentation confirming the story above, there is another story of legal proceedings against Stout. The only evidence of this action is a story told more than ninety years after the event supposedly occurred and from a book written even later.

During the annual meeting of the Tennessee Bar Association in July 1912, Colonel W. A. Henderson gave a speech to the body called "Chimney Corner Law." During the speech, Henderson delivered a highly entertaining account of Obed Stout's witch trial.

Henderson told his audience that Stout was "an old, little, misshapen man" of unknown origins. Stout had wandered along Cowan's Trace in Fentress County until he found a suitable place to live.

Stout soon came under suspicion from the local folk. It seems that the community suffered from epidemics, a drought had dried up streams and ravaged the land. The harvests were small and food became scarce. Beyond that, most of the children in Fentress County came down with measles. Many of the residents of the small, backwoods county believed that Stout was causing their misery. However, they were a patient lot.

The patience of the people in and around Jamestown ran out when a "young mountain girl" named Nancy Taylor declared that she was under a spell. Miss Taylor did not feel like going to church and she could not raise her voice – although she tried to shout several times. She had no appetite and she listlessly dragged herself around her home.

The case of Nancy Taylor was evidence, in the minds of the good folk of Fentress County of "vile conjury." Since the Taylor girl was, in their minds, bewitched, and since they believed that Stout was a wizard, there was no surprise when the men of the county arrested the little old man.

Believing the only way to exonerate a witch was through trial by ordeal, his accusers set up several tests for Stout to take. They designed the tests to cause him great pain and death.

First, they made Stout walk across searing hot plowshares. His did this without receiving burns. However, some witnesses later said that the plowshares did not burn Stout because he "hopped over them."

Next, his accusers threw Stout into a millpond, but he stubbornly refused to drown. Instead Stout waded out of the water "with much malice and aforethought."

Then, the good folk of Jamestown flogged Stout with hazel switches, but he was obstinate and he "refused to bleed."

Finally, his accusers forced Stout to drink a large helping of boiled rattlesnake weed thinking it would poison him. However, since rattlesnake weed tea is not poisonous, Stout survived.

Since Stout "failed" all the tests put before him, the townsfolk concluded that he was indeed under the influence of Satan.

The citizens of Jamestown decided to take Stout before a magistrate named Joshua Owen. However, before transporting him, the guards removed the lead balls from their rifles and replaced them with silver bullets.

The person chosen to prosecute Stout was a "neighborhood busybody" named Link Pelter. Pelter called several witnesses who testified that they had seen Stout escape from houses through keyholes in doors. One female witness testified that she had seen the little old man, or someone who looked like him, in the nighttime with wings on his shoulders. Other witnesses testified that several men who Stout had laid his eyes upon had fallen ill and that their "cattle and horses, and other stock, had sickened and died."

Stout remained silent through the proceedings and did not present a defense.

During his lecture, Henderson stated his opinion that "Stout himself was imbued with the idea that he really was a wizard of the most dangerous variety, because a wizard is a stewed witch, stewed out of an old bachelor."

Magistrate Owen declared Stout guilty and ordered him bound over to the Circuit Court. However, the Attorney General, John B. McCormick, refused to bring Stout to trial. The very embarrassed Attorney General sent Stout back home.

Angry at his shabby treatment, Stout sought an indictment against his persecutors for assault and battery. The state indicted several of those who had abused the little man.

Interestingly, those charged with assaulting Stout claimed that they had a right to do what they did. They stated that common law and English statutes, allowed for the torture of wizards. In fact, they contended that they were within their rights to inflict twice as much brutality upon Stout as they had had actually committed.

There were no specific laws against witchcraft in Tennessee. Thus, Stout's accusers relied upon British law to prosecute him. Stout's abusers pointed to the statutes of Henry VIII and James I making witchcraft a felony. They declared that Tennessee had never repealed the laws in question.

Judge Abraham Caruthers charged the jury that the statutes mentioned above were "repugnant to, and destructive freedom of the State, and a republican form of government."

The judge continued that that by the Act of 1778, the aforementioned statutes were never in effect in the Volunteer State. In addition, as we have seen, Great Britain outlawed the statutes of Henry VIII and James I in 1735.

The court convicted the persecutors and ordered them to pay damages. The decision to punish the witch hunters was very unpopular. In fact, when the judge announced the verdict, angry spectators almost caused a riot and the trial judge received death threats for years after that.

Henderson's speech, delivered in a lighthearted way decades after the alleged events, includes the only account of this particular accusation against Stout that the author has been able to locate – except for a short mention of it in the 1916 book *History of Fentress County* that listed the events as taking place in 1835.

It is likely that Henderson was repeating a corrupted version of the events of 1831. Proof of this is that Judge Caruthers, who was born in 1803, was not on the bench in 1820. Either way, it is certain that authorities hauled Obed Stout before a court at least once for being a witch. It is also certain that the court refused to convict him and that a court punished his accusers. It is great to know that sometimes justice trumps superstition.

12. American Witch Doctors

When one thinks of witch doctors (sometimes spelled "witchdoctor"), Africa and tropical islands may come to mind. However, here in Tennessee witch doctors practiced for many years.

Witch doctors were not witches or wizards themselves. On the contrary, they performed duties they thought would thwart witchery. They provided remedies to ward off evil spirits, they performed exorcisms, and they sometimes attempted to free buildings inhabited by ghosts and "haints."

Witch doctoring came to America, not from Africa, but from England. While witch doctoring had been around for much longer, the first recorded mention of English witch doctors occurred in the early 18th century. English theologian Francis Hutchinson mentioned witch doctors in an essay he wrote on witchcraft in 1718.

Hutchinson relayed an account of a woman named Dorothy Durent who testified during a witch trial. Durent stated that a witch doctor showed her how to catch a witch (in the form of a toad) in a blanket. She continued that when she put the toad in her fireplace it exploded. Hutchinson scoffed at the idea of witch doctors. He said Durent was a "silly, loose woman or she would not have gone to a witch doctor."

In days gone by, many Tennesseans considered witch doctors to practice a noble vocation and witch doctors passed their craft down from generation to generation. Of course, not everyone agreed. Many Tennesseans were like Hutchinson. They categorized witch doctors as quacks and charlatans.

Witch doctors practiced their trade in Tennessee long after the trial of Obed Stout. An account in a Nashville newspaper published on May 12, 1867 stated that a witch doctor from Smith County answered a call to come to Wilson County to drive a ghost from a smokehouse. The witch doctor fired silver bullets at the ghost "without effect."

13. Silver Bullets and Witches

Some of the trials in this book include references to silver bullets. The truth is that silver bullets – and other items fashioned from silver – played a major role in "capturing" and driving out witches.

Influenced by movies and the like, virtually everyone knows the legend of werewolves. The legend states that nothing can kill a werewolf but a bullet, or some other object fashioned from silver. Thus, in movies and popular fiction, werewolf hunters employ silver bullets.

However, most do not know that in past centuries those believing in supernatural things employed silver bullets against all types of mythical creatures. Some held that the silver bullet was the only method of killing a witch, a giant, a werewolf, a hobgoblin, or any person living a supernatural life. Some even believed that one could defeat a vampire with silver bullets – under the right conditions.

In the early 19th century, the Brothers Grimm related a fairy tale called *The Two Brothers* in which the heroes used silver bullets to kill a witch.

Why use silver bullets? In western culture, silver was associated with darkness and the moon, while gold was associated with light and the sun. Thus, it makes some sense that witch doctors would use silver against creatures of the night. Beyond that, in the Dark Ages, physicians discovered that silver had certain limited medicinal qualities. Thus, it made sense that silver bullets could "cure" supernatural beings.

Silver bullets remained a staple in the arsenal of witch finders for as long as the practice of hunting down exterminating witches was common.

14. The One-Eyed Witch

Witch trials diminished as the nineteenth century worn on, but the belief in the Black Arts persisted. While slavery, tariffs, or other sectional disputes ripping at the fabric of the nation concerned most citizens, a few Americans still worried that witches were running amok.

The witch trial covered in this chapter took place in North Central Arkansas in 1858 or 1859. While the author has not located written records of the event, the stories handed down orally have a ring of truth to them.

It seems that a woman called "Old Mrs. Inman" found herself accused of witchcraft. Inman, who was blind in one eye, lived just east of Alpena, Arkansas at a place called "Lick Branch."

In either 1858 or 1859, a young woman named Gaddy went before the Primitive Baptist Church in what is now Dunkard community. The community was then in Carroll County, but later Boone County annexed it. Miss Gaddy accused Mrs. Inman of witchery before the congregation. Inman denied that she was a witch.

As it seems was with case with other Primitive Baptist churches, this one was keenly interested in a complaint of witchcraft filed against one of its members. The congregation agreed to investigate the matter and hold a trial to determine what action, if any, it should take against Inman.

At a regular monthly session of church, Miss Gaddy came before the congregation and testified against Old Mrs. Inman. Gaddy told the enraptured congregation a vivid story. She said that Inman came to her house on several occasions, saddled and bridled her, then rode her "for miles over the hills and valleys of Carroll County."

As strange as the mental image of Old Mrs. Inman riding Miss Gaddy was, Gaddy added a startling and disgusting detail. Gaddy told her fellow churchgoers that once Inman did something much worse than simply riding her. Miss Gaddy testified that on one dark evening Inman rode her into a neighbor's barn and forced her to have sexual relations with a Spanish donkey. One can only imagine the gasps released by the congregation at the thought of Old Mrs. Inman forcing Miss Gaddy to engage in bestiality with a farm animal.

How could one answer Gaddy's testimony logically? One could not. Inman had no positive evidence to refute Gaddy's testimony. How could she provide any? The best she could do was to deny the charges and to rely on her Godly character to cause the congregation to acquit her. It was not enough.

The congregation simply could not get past their repulsion of Inman that Gaddy's shocking and disturbing testimony engendered. Had they considered the ridiculous charges with logic, they would have acquitted Inman, but their emotions ruled them.

The church members considered the matter for a short time and then they voted to excommunicate Inman. Then the church members attempted to put the sordid matter behind them and forget it.

15. The "Old Hag Syndrome"

Interestingly, there are many stories of witches coming to their victims at night and riding them. These cases are all similar in that the victim feels the presence of a supernatural being upon his or her chest.

The work titled "De ecclesiasticis disciplinis" from the year 906 ascribed to the Roman Catholic churchman Regino von Prüm mentioned a similar and common experience akin to witch riding. He wrote that "certain abandoned women, turning aside to follow Satan, being seduced by the illusions and phantasms of demons, believe and openly profess that in the dead of night they ride upon certain beasts along with the pagan goddess Diana and a countless horde of women and that in these silent hours they fly over vast tracts of country and obey her as their mistress, while on other nights they are summoned to pay her homage."

Medical professionals have discovered that these feelings of visitation from a supernatural being have a natural explanation. The "Old Hag Syndrome" (more commonly called "sleep paralysis" by medical professionals) is rather common. It occurs most often during a sudden transition between deep sleep and awakening.

Common symptoms of sleep paralysis include the inability to move and vivid hallucinations. While sleep paralysis typically lasts for only a few seconds, it can seem to last for hours.

Old Hag Syndrome is a form of sleep disorder that medical professionals can successfully treat.

Considering her testimony from the above chapter, Miss Gaddy may well have been suffering from sleep paralysis. If Miss Gaddy *was* a victim of the disorder, she could have honestly believed that Old Mrs. Inman was coming to her at night, riding her, and forcing her to perform grotesque acts.

Again, if she suffered from the malady of sleep paralysis, Miss Gaddy could have stood before the church assembly and told a story that she thought was completely true. Under those conditions, Gaddy would likely have been very convincing. Of course, in those days, few persons had any interest in medical explanations of supposed enchantments and they were more than willing to accept a supernatural explanation of the events Miss Gaddy described.

16. European Witch Trials

Witch Trials did not originate in America, of course. The settlers of North America imported many things, including the fear of witches and the desire to find and stamp out witchery wherever it arose. This being the case, one cannot understand American witch trials without taking a brief look at previous trials in Europe.

The belief in witchcraft is as old as civilization. There were stories of demons aided by witches and sorcerers long before the writings of Moses and other Old Testament authors. There are mentions of in several places. For instance, the Code of the Babylonian king Hammurabi (about 2000 BC) states:

"If a man has laid a charge of witchcraft and has not justified it, he upon whom the witchcraft is laid shall go to the holy river; he shall plunge into the holy river and if the holy river overcome him, he who accused him shall take to himself his house."

Biblical authors added to, and expanded upon, the idea of witchcraft. To some theologians, witchcraft became a major facet of their faith. The Roman Catholic Church viewed witchcraft as involving "the idea of a diabolical pact, or at least an appeal to the intervention of the spirits of evil." Catholic leaders believed that these appeals involved requests to cause injury or death to opponents, cause someone to fall in love, or to reanimate the dead.

The Catholics thought that witches and wizards made compacts with Satan or his minions and that these witches promised to perform evil acts in exchange for the demented power offered by the forces of darkness. Some of the specific acts the Catholic Church accused witches of performing included:

(1) Renouncing Jesus and the Sacraments

(2) Observing the Witches' Sabbath

(3) Performing "infernal rites" including the "Black Mass"

(4) Paying "divine honor" to the "Prince of Darkness"

In exchange for their devotion to Satan, witches and wizards believed – according to the Roman Catholics – that they would gain among other things:

(1) The ability to fly

(2) The ability to change shapes

(3) Imps and "familiar spirits" to aid them in any way they desired

With the rise if the Roman Catholic Church within the Roman Empire, the line between church and state blurred. In fact, it is sometimes difficult to determine where one ends and the other begins. Thus, it is difficult to tell if civil or church authorities carried on certain of the persecutions against suspected witches.

The power of the Church continued throughout Europe after the fall of Rome. Then, when Protestant sects replaced the

Catholic Church in some nations, those sects held great sway politically as well. Nowhere was church power more prevalent than in the attempts to overcome the perceived influence of witchcraft.

Perhaps due to Christian influence, in the third century, the Roman Empire passed a law to counteract witches. This legislation mandated the burning alive of any witch that caused the death of another through enchantment.

The Roman Catholic Church became involved with witchcraft officially at the Council of Elvira in 306. The council voted to refuse Holy Communion to any person who had killed another by the use of a spell. The council reasoned that one could not commit such a crime without the use of idolatry and devil-worship.

In 314, the Council of Ancyra placed a penalty of five years of penance on anyone that consulted with a magician. The reasoning behind this action was that the Catholic Church associated magic with paganism. The legislation of the Council of Ancyra remained the Catholic position for several centuries. The Council of Trullo of 692 adopted similar penalties for magic.

In Ireland, the Catholic Church treated sorcery as a crime and excommunicated those involved with it until they had performed adequate penance.

As time passed, the Roman Catholic Church increased the severity of the penalties it inflicted on witches. The Council of Paderborn in 785 ordered the reduction of sorcerers to serfdom. In addition, the council decreed that "Whosoever, blinded by the devil and infected with pagan errors, holds another person for a witch that eats human flesh, and therefore burns her, eats her flesh, or gives it to others to eat, shall be punished with death."

Some church leaders attempted to convince the public that witchcraft was not real. However, the church never abandoned its efforts to exclude those claiming to be witches. Roman civil law permitted torture to exact confessions from suspected witches and while Pope Nicholas I decried torture in 866, the practice continued.

A good many Catholic leaders professed a disbelief in witchcraft, but the Church itself did not abandon the belief. For instance, around 1020, the Bishop of Worms professed a continued belief that witches could produce magical potions that could cause such things as impotence and abortions. However, he claimed that he did not believe that witches could fly, control the forces of nature, or transform humans into beasts. Neither did he believe that humans could have sexual intercourse with supernatural beings. However, he did believe that attempts to perform those acts were sinful, and, therefore, subject to physical punishment.

False accusations of witchcraft, and the severe punishment these accusations caused, led church leaders to act. In 1080, Pope Gregory VII ordered King Harold of Denmark to stop executing witches on the charges that they caused storms, crop failures, or pestilence. However, the Pope did not forbid the burning of witches for other crimes.

The persecution of suspected witches did not decline with time – it grew worse. By the middle of the thirteenth century, the Papal Inquisition was investigating witchcraft and punishing witches. Pope Alexander VI proclaimed in 1258 that the Inquisitors should only concern themselves with heretical beliefs. However, since the church considered almost any suspected practice of magic to be heresy, witchcraft was a subject for the Inquisition from the beginning.

The Roman Catholic Church considered the Cathar and the Manichaean faiths as both heretical and associated with black magic. Thus, the Inquisition assumed that all members of those faiths were likely witches. It is no surprise that a very early witch burning took place in Toulouse, France. Toulouse was a center of the Cathar faith and inquisitor, Hugues de Baniol, ordered a woman burned at the stake there in 1275.

The woman the inquisitor ordered burned had confessed to her crimes after suffering through several sessions of intense torture. She admitted giving birth to a great monster after she had sexual relations with an "evil spirit." Then, she stated that she kept her monster alive by feeding it with the flesh of babies that she had kidnapped during her many nighttime excursions.

As ridiculous as the ideal of sexual relations between humans and demons may sound to us, many early church leaders viewed such intercourse as an undeniable fact. Among those church leaders believing that humans and demons could procreate were St. Thomas Aquinas and St. Bonaventure.

Others did not believe in women flying through the air, and transforming themselves into demons. These men considered such persons claiming to do such things as "heathen nonsensical impostures." Yet, these same people felt that the imposters were committing "one of the greatest sins" and that they deserved severe punishment.

During the fourteenth century Popes John XXIII and Benedict XII encouraged inquisitors to persecute those accused of being witches. In 1334, at a large witch trial at Toulouse there were several persons burned and fifty-five others imprisoned for either life or long terms. Two of those sentenced to death were elderly women who broke under long hours of torture and confessed. They admitted they had assisted in witches' Sabbaths, had worshipped Satan, had intercourse with him, and had eaten the flesh of babies they had carried off in the night.

Ten years before the case above, a person named Petronilla de Midia suffered death by burning at the stake in Ireland by order of the Bishop of Ossory.

In addition to the church, civil authorities in Europe also meted out severe punishment against witches. Some of the earliest civil laws prohibited the practice of witchcraft. For instance, the legal code called the "Salic Law" published by the Franks in the early 6th century forbade witchery.

The secular courts also practiced torture and burned witches at the stake. However, it is sometimes very difficult to determine if a secular or religious authorities initiated a given witch trial – or if the persecution was a combined effort by both. About 1400, Peter de Gruyeres prosecuted many, many suspected witches in Berne, Switzerland. While some sources claim that the Catholic Church mandated the trials, others claim they were the result of civil actions.

Some of the most brutal witch punishments were unquestionably the acts of civil authorities. Civil persecutions in Valais, Switzerland between 1428 and 1434 led to the execution of around 200 persons suspected of witchcraft. The suspected witches – two-thirds of whom were men – faced charges of murder, heresy, sorcery, making pacts with, and paying tributes to, the Devil. Under torture, several of those suspected confessed to causing lameness, blindness, madness, miscarriage, impotence, infertility, and of killing and eating their own children. Variations of these same charges were applied during witch trials everywhere such trials took place.

Another large civil action against suspected witches took place in France in 1437. More than 150 suffered punishment, some of them by drowning.

However, the fact that civil authorities ratcheted up its persecution of suspected witches does not mean that the Catholic

Church was still. Church Inquisitions were very active in places such as Heidelberg in 1447 and Savoy in 1462. The various Inquisitions oversaw the executions of many suspected witches.

In France, the inquisitors came to refer to suspected witches as the "Vauderie." The term grew to such prominence that it became a recognized legal term meaning "Sorcery; witchcraft; the profession of the Vaudois."

Roman Catholic hegemony over Europe gave way to a large and active Protestant movement. However, the Protestants were no more tolerant of suspected witches than were the Catholics. Protestant leaders agreed that witchcraft and other magical practices enhanced the power of the Devil. Martin Luther was adamant that that witches should suffer extermination.

In 1532, the German Empire adopted the Code of Carolina. The law declared sorcery as a criminal offense and it contained a provision for burning at the stake any witch that harmed another person.

Beginning in about 1563, religious leaders began to criticize the wanton abuse of accused witches. However, the critics did not have much impact on the persecution. On the contrary, authorities expanded penalties for witchery as time went along. In 1572, Augustus of Saxony imposed burning at the stake for every form of witchcraft, including fortune telling.

Witch trials continued throughout the 16th century. In the German town of Osnabrück, in 1583, authorities burned 121 persons in a three-month span. In addition, in 1593, authorities in Wolfenbutten1 burned as many as ten accused witches each day.

Witch trials and executions spread to England and Scotland. The only real difference between witch trials in English speaking countries and the rest of Europe was the method of killing accused witches. In Great Britain, the authorities preferred hanging to burning.

It is uncertain how many accused witches authorities executed in Great Britain, but it was a large number. During the reign of Oliver Cromwell (a Puritan), estimates of hanging of accused witches range from 3,000 to 30,000. The 30,000 number is certainly too high. The entire population of England in 1650 was only 4,200,000. It is impossible that Cromwell's cronies killed almost one percent of the population of England for any reason, much less witchcraft. Regardless of the exact number, a large number of English citizens did suffer at the hands of Cromwell's witch hunters.

Matthew Hopkins grew famous for aiding the Cromwell regime in chasing down witches. Hopkins grew so proud of his work that he labeled himself "Witchfinder General." However, an associate of Hopkins named John Stearne may have been the most successful witch hunter in Great Britain. Stearne bragged of tracking down at least 200 witches and witnessing their execution.

Another writer claimed that around 1648, 300 witches went on trial in Essex and Suffolk over a two-year timeframe. The writer claimed that most of accused witches went to the gallows.

Witch trials were also common in Scotland. A report published two centuries later claimed that 3,400 suspected witches went to the gallows at the height of the Scottish witch mania. Of course, such a high number is impossible for a nation with a population as small as that of Scotland, but the report does prove that the flaming fear of witchery ensnared many persons there as well.

Long after America's most notorious bout of hysteria associated with witchcraft had burned itself out, witch trials in Europe continued. Several European cities and states outlawed torturing witches in the late 18th and early 19th century (Prussia in 1754, Bavaria in 1807, Hanover in 1822). However, the fact that authorizes outlawed torture indicates that they intended to continue to hold witch trials. They simply intended to be gentler with the persons they accused.

Some sources contend that before the end of the European witch trials 110,000 persons went on trial for witchcraft and that between 40,000 to 60,000 of them died at the hands of executioners. These numbers are greatly inflated. However, there is no doubt that many thousands suffered persecution while the witch trials rumbled through medieval Europe.

17. The Salem Myths

It is the author's hope that this little book will help explode some of the myths about witch trials. Since the infamous Salem witch trials are the best known, and most related of the American witch trials, most refer to them as a basis for their beliefs concerning all American witch trials. Therefore, it is easy to see why myths about witch trials grew up due to the events in Salem.

The Trials in Salem

In order to understand the myths of Salem, one must understand the Salem trials. Therefore, a brief look at the trials is necessary.

The trials took place in Salem Village (now Danvers), Massachusetts between June 1692 and May 1693.

Salem Village (not to be confused with the larger Salem Town, which we know today as Salem) was a small, rather poor community of about 500 citizens. Two families dominated Salem Village, the somewhat well to do Porters and the marginally poorer Putnam family. The two families were rivals in many matters and most of the townsfolk aligned themselves with one family or the other.

In 1689, the Putnam family influenced the Salem Village Congregational Church to hire Samuel Parris as its new pastor. Parris was from Boston originally. He was charming and well read. He studied at Harvard, but he never graduated. Parris had participated in modestly successful business enterprises, but he felt called to the church. Parris came to Salem Village with his wife, their three children, a niece, and two slaves. One of the slaves was a woman called Tituba.

When Parris took over the church at Salem Village, the community was suffering through "hard times." The aftereffects of a recent war between Great Britain and France harmed the town's economy. Additionally a smallpox epidemic had recently devastated the town, and the residents feared that an attack from hostile tribes of Native Americans was imminent. Beyond all that, the citizens of Salem Village believed that the wealthy business leaders of the nearby Salem Town were actively harming them economically.

After a short time as Pastor, Samuel Parris, who was middle-aged, felt discontented. The folk at his church had contracted to pay him a good wage for seeing to the affairs of the church, but soon he felt he needed more money to live in the comfort he deserved. However, he felt trapped in his contract.

With all its problems Salem Village suffered from growing tensions. This being the case, it would not take much to cause an eruption of anger and hatred in the small town. The eruption occurred in January 1692. It took a form no one could have imagined.

In January 1692, Pastor Parris found two members of his household strangely ill. His 9-year-old daughter Elizabeth (Betty) and his niece, 11-year-old Abigail Williams began to suffer from "fits." Among other things, the girls experienced violent spasms, contortions, writhing, and uncontrollable screaming.

Parris called in local physician, William Griggs to diagnose and cure the children. Griggs was stumped. Without a scientific explanation for the illness, Griggs concluded that the children suffered bewitchment.

Within a month, several other girls began displaying similar symptoms. Among these afflicted girls were Ann Putnam Jr., Mercy Lewis, Elizabeth Hubbard, Mary Walcott, and Mary Warren.

By late February, some of the children had identified three women they claimed had bewitched them. The women included a beggar named Sarah Good and an elderly woman named Sarah Osborne. However, the leading suspect was the female slave Parris held in bondage. Her name was Tituba. The authorities issued warrants for the three and they appeared before magistrates Jonathan Corwin and John Hathorne.

While the magistrates questioned the accused women, the chief accusers brought the afflicted girls into the courtroom. The children made a display of fits that few persons had ever seen in public before. Though almost everyone in the courtroom now believed the three women were guilty, Good and Osborn proclaimed their innocence.

On the other hand, Tituba admitted to her guilt. Not only that, Tituba volunteered to implicate other witches. She said there were several members of the community of Salem Village working in concert with the Devil.

Soon, witch mania gripped Salem Village. However, the hysteria did not end at the town limits. It spilled into other parts of Massachusetts as well. Accusations flew wildly and eventually reached upstanding members of the church and even extended the Sarah Good's four-year-old daughter Dorothy.

Several accused witches confessed and named others. Soon, the local court system had more cases than it was possible to handle. In May 1692, William Phips, the new Royal Governor of the Massachusetts Bay Colony, created a new court whose only function was to hear and decide witch cases in Suffolk, Essex and Middlesex counties. The justices of this court included John Hathorne, Samuel Sewall, and William Stoughton.

The witch court handed down its first conviction on Monday, June 2, 1692 when it determined that Bridget Bishop was guilty. She hung for her "crimes" eight days later. After the hanging of Bishop, the executions picked up over the next three months. Those hung included:

July 19, 1692: Sarah Good, Elizabeth Howe, Susannah Martin, and Sarah Wildes;

August 19, 1692: George Burroughs, George Jacobs, Sr., Martha Carrier, John Proctor, and John Willard;

September 22, 1692: Martha Corey, Mary Eastery, Mary Parker, Alice Parker, Ann

Pudeator, Wilmont Redd, Margaret Scott, and Samuel Wardell.

In addition, on September 19, 1692, the authorities placed large rocks on Giles Corey (husband of Martha Corey) in order to compel him to enter a plea on the charges of witchcraft. He never entered a plea and the rocks pressed him to death.

Beyond those who experienced execution by hanging or weight, at least five others died in custody. These included Ann Foster, Lyndia Dustin, Mercy (enfant daughter of Sarah Good), Sarah Osborn and Roger Toothaker.

Respected minister Cotton Mather and his father, President of Harvard, Increase Mather believed in witches. Yet, they both condemned convicting witches based on "spectral evidence" (evidence based on dreams, visions, or other things that had no basis in reality). They held that evidence for witchcraft must be equal to those for any other crime. Increase Mather went so far as to state his opinion that "It would better that ten suspected witches may escape than one innocent person be condemned."

In October 1692, Governor Phips dissolved the special court and mandated that the one court replacing it refuse to accept spectral evidence.

Like all bouts of fever, the witch mania in Massachusetts ran its fitful course, eventually. Witch Trials continued until early 1693, but no one suffered execution after September 1692. Finally, by May 1693, Governor Phips pardoned and released all those in prison on witchcraft charges.

The trials came to be an embarrassment to the Massachusetts Bay Colony. In January 1697, the Massachusetts General Court (legislature) declared a day of fasting for the tragedy of the Salem witch trials. Later, the General Court declared the trials unlawful. In addition, one of the leading justices, Samuel Sewall, publicly apologized for his role in the process.

Now for the Myths

Several myths grew up based on the Salem trials and the popular fiction written about them. Below are a few of the myths.

(1) Authorities only charge women with witchery. Of course, this book relates the story of the alleged Tennessee Wizard, Obed Stout. In addition, if one takes a look at those hung in Salem, he will find that six of the nineteen were men.

(2) Another myth that this book debunks is that those charged with witchcraft could not receive a fair trial. The truth is that most of those charged with witchery – at least in the southland – did get fair trials and most received acquittals. Some even received damages from their accusers.

(3) Another myth is that accusations of witchery invariably led to mass hysteria. This was certainly true in Salem, but not elsewhere. Of the nine southern cases related in this book, none of them led to hysteria, or to mass arrests.

(4) Another myth is that accused witches remained ostracized for the remainder of their days. While this was true in some cases, but it was just as likely that the accusers became outcasts.

The author could add other items to this list, but the above should provide enough evidence to cause the reader to ignore the myths when researching witch trials conducted in the United States.

Conclusion

"First they came for the Socialists, and I did not speak out — Because I was not a Socialist. Then they came for the Trade Unionists, and I did not speak out — Because I was not a Trade Unionist. Then they came for the Jews, and I did not speak out — Because I was not a Jew. Then they came for me —and there was no one left to speak for me." – Attributed to Martin Niemöller

While it was the author's intent to entertain the reader with these witch trial stories from the southern United States – he intended to do more than that. He endeavored to show that a look at these trials gives us insight into our present times. The trials related here correlate well with our current – seemly confused – national environment.

We should not dismiss the southern witch trials – no matter how gentle many of them may have been – as footnotes of history, or as the delusions of superstitious and ignorant frontiersmen. The trials say something about human actions and reactions when faced with things they do not readily understand. Irrational fear leads to irrational acts, and irrational acts lead to violent persecution. It does not matter if the subject of the irrational fear are witches, are members of a different race, a different religion, a different political belief, or any other difference. The result of irrational fear is always persecution and persecution is never justified.

In addition, there are always demagogues who are more than willing to exploit irrational fears to pursue their own cruel ambitions. These persons are the real evil ones – the real monsters among us. They are the ones against whom we should guard ourselves. Because if we allow others to suffer persecution – whether or not we take part in it directly – we are opening ourselves, and our families, to similar persecutions down the road.

No ideology has the moral high ground when it comes to intolerance. Political liberals, conservatives and everyone else are sometimes intolerant with those who express views differing from theirs.

By the time intolerance becomes destructive, it is often too late to stop it. Nazi Germany and Communist Russia are the two examples that come readily to mind, but intolerance has been a destructive force in practically every nation and practically every society. It is always present, always bubbling – like a witch's cauldron – just below the surface, ready to boil over at any time.

Sources Consulted

Bently, James. *Martin Niemöller: 1892–1984*. New York: Macmillan Free Press, 1984.

Blackstone, William. *Commentaries on the Laws of England*. Oxford: Clarendon Press, 1765-1769.

Bruce, Philip Alexander. *Intuitional History of Virginia in the Seventeenth Century, Volume I*. New York: G. P. Putnam's Sons, 1910.

Burr, George Lincoln. *Narratives of the Witchcraft Cases: 1648-1706*. New York: Charles Scribner's Sons, 1914.

Constitution of the Presbyterian Church, The: Containing the Confession of Faith, The Larger and Shorter Catechisms, as Ratified by the General Assembly. Richmond, Virginia: Whittet and Shepperson, 1910.

Davies, Owen. *Witchcraft, Magic and Culture, 1736-1951*. Manchester and New York: Manchester University Press, 1999.

Davis, Richard Beale "The Devil in Virginia in the Seventeenth Century" *Virginia Magazine of History and Biography 65* (1957) pages 131-49

Demos, John Putnam. *Entertaining Satan: Witchcraft and Culture of Early New England*. Oxford: Oxford University Press; Updated Edition, 2004.

Drake, Frederick C. "Witchcraft in the American Colonies, 1647-62" *American*

Quarterly, Volume 20, No. 4 (Winter, 1968), pages 694-725.

Edwards, Cyrus and Florence Edwards Gardiner. *Cyrus Edwards' Stories of Early Days and Others*. Standard Printing Company, 1940.

Gandee, Lee R. "The Witches of Fairfield, S.C." *FATE*. January 1970, pages 36-44.

"Ghost in Wilson County." *Nashville Union and Dispatch*, May 12, 1867

Gorin, Sandra K. *A DECEMBER 1813 WITCHCRAFT TRIAL IN NOW HART CO KY*. Posted on May 31, 2011. (Retrieved from: http://searches2.rootsweb.com/th/read/KENTUCKY-LEGENDS/2011-05/1306843216)

Grimm, Wilhelm and Jacob Grimm. Margaret Hunt, Translator. *The Complete Folk and Fairy Tales of the Brothers Grimm*. Stockholm, Sweden: Wisehouse Classics, 2016.

Gross, Samuel and Maurice Pasley. "Why do People Confess to Crimes they didn't Commit?" *Newsweek*, June 16, 2016.

Hopkins, Matthew. *The Discovery of Witches*. Qontro Classic Books (reprint), 2010.

Mather, Cotton and Increase Mather. *The Wonders of the Invisible World - Being an Account of the Tryals of Several Witches Lately - Executed in New-England, to which is added A Farther Account - of the Tryals of the New-England Witches*. London: John Russell Smith, 1862 (reprint).

Henderson, W. A. "Chimney Corner Law," a speech given during the *Proceedings of the*

Annual Session of the Bar Association of Tennessee. Knoxville: July 9-11, 1912.

Heuffer, Oliver Madox. *The Book of Witches*. New York: The John McBride Co., 1909.

Holy Bible, The: Commonly Known as the Authorized (King James) Version. Public Domain Work issued by many publishers

Houge, A. R. *History of Fentress County: The Old Home of Mark Twain's Ancestors*. Nashville: Williams Printing Company, 1916.

Hutchinson, Francis. *An Historical Essay Concerning Witchcraft*. London: Printed for R. Knaplock and D. Midwinter, 1718.

Monaster, Antoine. *A History of the Vaudois Church*. New York: Lane and Scott, 1849.

Poulson's American Daily Advertiser (Philadelphia), August 10, 1834.

Royal, Anne Newport. *Letters From Alabama on Various Subjects*. Washington, D. C., 1830.

Sakowski, Carolyn. *Touring the East Tennessee Backroads*. Winston-Salem, North Carolina: John F. Blair, 1993.

Saunders, James Edmonds. *Early Settlers of Alabama*. New Orleans: L. Graham and Son, 1899.

Scott, Betty M. (Project Coordinator). *Macon County, Tennessee History and Families*. Paducah, Kentucky: Turner Publishing Company, 2001. Published by the Macon County, Tennessee Historical Society.

Scott, Betty M. "Testament Baptist Church." *Macon County Historical Society Newsletter, Volume 1, Issue 3*, September 1985, pages 7-8.

Starkey, Marion L. *The Devil in Massachusetts: A Modern Enquiry into the Salem Witch Trials.* New York: Time, 1949.

Thurston, Herbert. "Witchcraft." *The Catholic Encyclopedia, Vol. 15*. New York: Robert Appleton Company, 1912.

Vance, Randolph. "Witch Trial in Carroll County." *The Arkansas Historical Quarterly, Vol. 16, No. 1 (Spring, 1957)*, pages 89-90.

Walser, Richard. *The North Carolina Miscellany.* New York: Van Rees Press, 1962.

Wheeler, John H. *Reminiscences and Memoirs of North Carolina and Eminent North Carolinians.* Columbus, Ohio: Columbus Printing Works, 1884.

White, Newman Ivey, General Editor. *The Frank C. Broom Collection of North Carolina Folklore, Volume VII.* Durham, North Carolina: Duke University Press, 1964.

"Witchcraft." *Nashville Herald*, July 22, 1831.

"Witchcraft." *New York Evening Post*, August 8, 1831.

About the Author

CL Gammon has had a life-long fascination with American History and with the written word. These joint fascinations have led to his becoming an award winning and an internationally known bestselling author of more than thirty books. Gammon, who studied Political Science at Tennessee Technological University and History and Government at Hillsdale College, has entertained and educated readers for more than a decade. Several universities, including the State University of New York and the University of Akron, have used his books as course material. In addition, articles written by Gammon have appeared in more than a dozen publications. Gammon lives in Lafayette, Tennessee with his family.

Other Books by CL Gammon

CL Gammon has written books covering many topics including history, politics, sports, and fiction. They include:

Abraham Lincoln: Warrior in Chief

Alexander Hamilton's Plan for America

America's First Rules of War

America's Fourteen Presidents

America's Other Party: A Brief History of the Prohibition Party

A Revolutionary War Cookbook (And More)

Bad Football Saturday's 50 Worst Teams Ever!

Bizarre Murders in Tennessee: 13 True Stories

Expelling the Senate's Gentlemen Traitors

Guns, Politics and Independence

Hail to the Chief: The Presidency by the Numbers

Hanging the Macon County Witch

Jefferson Davis Rallies the Rebels (1863)

Make Sure You are Right, then Go Ahead and other Essays

McGovern-Eagleton '72: A Crazy Train Wreck

Nazi Mad Science I: High Altitude Experiments

Seven Candidates for President in 1972

Simon the Accuser: A Christian Novel

The American Presidents: Briefly

The Big Fire (A novel)

The Continental Congress: America's Forgotten Government

The Great Mormon War of 1857-1858

The Great New Hampshire Primary Myth

The Hampton Roads Conference

The Macon County Race War

The Philosophy of the Confederate Constitution

The Politics of the Crucifixion

The Preamble of the United States Constitution

The Story of the First Continental Congress

The True Story of Axis Sally

Ultimate Penalty: Executing Robert Glen Coe

Ultimate Penalty II: Executing Sedley Alley

Was Lucille Ball a Communist?

Why Johnson Created the Warren Commission

Why the Articles of Confederation Failed

Made in United States
Orlando, FL
02 November 2023